Contents

"The function of good software is to make the complex appear to be simple." — Grady Booch

— Grady Booch

1. An Ode to System Administration: The Unseen Art of Process Management

In the realm of system administration, where commands become spells that conjure optimally running servers, mastering the process tree on a Linux system is akin to perfecting the art of bonsai. Just as the bonsai artist carefully trims branches to shape a healthy and aesthetically pleasing miniature tree, so too must a system administrator understand, monitor, and, when necessary, kill processes to maintain an efficient and stable operating environment. But why delve into the intricate dance of threads, memory allocations, and runtime binaries?

Imagine a maze of operations, each path leading to tasks as diverse as handling user requests, processing computations, and managing network traffic. Within this labyrinth, 'Top' emerges as the magical lens, providing a dynamic, real-time view of these concurrent processes. Although 'Top' is fundamentally a powerful snapshot of system activity, the wisdom lies in knowing how to wield its capabilities effectively, pruning away unnecessary processes while nurturing those critical to your server's mission.

This book embarks on a journey through the Linux process tree, a quest not just to harness 'Top' but to transcend its basic use, equipping you with the knowledge to sculpt a responsive, agile system. As you navigate through chapters packed with technical insights, practical guides, and theoretical foundations, you will discover the elegance and necessity of mastery in process management, transforming complexity into simplicity. In your hands, the art of process-pruning will become as second nature as tending to a bonsai, and the Linux system will be your flourishing masterpiece.

2. Understanding the Linux Process

2.1. Introduction to Processes

Processes in a Linux system, akin to the intricate veins of a tree, form the lifeblood of computing tasks, enabling resources to be allocated efficiently and user commands to be executed seamlessly. These processes are not mere artifacts of the operating system; they represent the active, dynamic interactions between software and hardware, translating user actions into computable tasks. To understand the significance of processes is to grasp the very essence of how a Linux environment operates.

At its core, a process is an instance of a running program, encompassing an ordered set of instructions, its own allocated memory, and a unique identifier known as a Process ID (PID). Each process in Linux operates within its own space, creating a manageable layer of abstraction that allows multiple processes to run concurrently without interference. This division is critical in maintaining system stability and security, as it encapsulates the execution context of each program. When a user opens a terminal to run a script, the system initiates a process that manages the script's execution, resource usage, and communication until it completes or is terminated.

However, the significance of processes extends beyond mere execution. Processes are managed according to specific states that reflect their current activity within the system's lifecycle. A running process might be in a 'running' state, actively utilizing CPU resources, or it might be 'waiting,' on hold for input from the user or responses from I/O operations. Moreover, processes can transition between various states as they execute, indicating their behavior over time. Understanding these states is crucial for effective system administration, as it allows administrators to optimize performance by identifying processes that may need termination or modification.

In Linux, processes exhibit unique characteristics that dictate their management. Each process is assigned a PID, which acts as a unique identifier allowing the system to track and manipulate it efficiently.

Parallel to this, a parent-child relationship exists between processes, where a parent process spawns one or more child processes. This hierarchical structure fosters modular programming, as processes can delegate tasks and communicate within their framework. For instance, a web server may spawn child processes to handle each incoming request, ensuring that the parent remains responsive while distributing workload effectively.

Additionally, the significance of processes lies in their role in resource management. Each process consumes system resources, including CPU cycles, memory, and disk I/O. When multiple processes compete for limited resources, the potential for bottlenecks arises, leading to system sluggishness or crashes. Effective resource allocation involves continuous monitoring and tuning of processes to ensure that critical tasks receive the necessary attention while potentially unnecessary ones are minimized or pruned from the process tree. Through tools like 'Top,' administrators gain insight into running processes, allowing them to make informed decisions about resource distribution, process prioritization, and system health.

As we move deeper into the exploration of processes within the Linux framework, the interaction between processes will unveil fascinating insights into system performance and reliability. Each chapter of this book aims to build on these foundations, guiding you through advanced techniques for process management, from understanding the nuances of inter-process communication to exploring the intricacies of process lifecycle management in a multi-core environment.

In rallying our efforts to cultivate mastery over Linux process management, we embark on a journey that promises to equip system administrators with the knowledge and skills needed to meticulously prune the process tree, fostering systems that run with the grace and efficiency of a well-tended bonsai. Through this complex yet rewarding landscape, you will learn not only to manage processes but to appreciate their dynamic interconnectivity, transforming how you interface with and maintain your Linux environments.

2.2. Process Characteristics

The intricate world of processes in a Linux operating system can be likened to a complex ecosystem where various entities interact, compete, and cooperate in a synchronized dance. To truly understand this ecosystem, it's essential to delve into the characteristics of processes themselves — their states, IDs, lifecycles, and how they collectively contribute to the stability and performance of the entire system.

At a fundamental level, every process begins as a program that has been loaded into memory for execution. Once the program is initiated, it assumes a process state that conveys critical information about its current activity within the operating system. The primary states of a process can be categorized as running, waiting (or sleeping), and stopped, each representing a vital part of the process's lifecycle. Understanding these states is crucial not only for system monitoring but also for optimizing performance.

In the running state, a process is actively utilizing CPU resources to perform tasks. However, the nature of multitasking operating systems requires that not all processes can run simultaneously due to limited CPU resources. Consequently, some processes may enter a waiting state, where they wait for external events such as I/O operations to complete or semaphore signals from other processes. This waiting mechanism is fundamental for ensuring that processes efficiently utilize CPU time while avoiding conflicts or resource starvation.

Processes are uniquely identified by their Process IDs (PIDs), which serve as the essential identifiers within the operating system's process table. Each PID is unique to its corresponding process during that process's existence. The management of PIDs is crucial for ensuring smooth operation within the system, allowing various commands and utilities, including 'Top' and 'ps,' to track and manage processes effectively. As system administrators, the ability to reference processes by their PIDs facilitates monitoring and manipulation, enabling actions such as pausing, terminating, or altering priorities with precision and confidence.

Moreover, the lifecycle of a process is comprised of several stages, ranging from its creation to its eventual termination. Upon invocation, a process is born through a series of steps that encompass resource allocation, initialization, and execution. In the creation phase, a parent process often invokes a child process through system calls like `fork()`, which duplicates the parent's current state, allowing the new process to inherit resources but operate independently. This forking mechanism creates a hierarchical relationship that is pivotal in understanding how processes manage tasks.

As processes execute, they may transition through different states based on their actions and interactions. For instance, a process may enter a suspended state if it is temporarily halted by the operating system or due to external factors. When processes finish their execution, they enter the terminated state, at which point the system reclaims their allocated resources. Notably, the termination phase is crucial for preventing resource leaks that could lead to system slowdown or crashes over time. An effective administrator can utilize tools to monitor these transitions, ensuring that orphaned processes are dealt with appropriately.

Inter-process relationships also contribute to understanding process characteristics. Processes exist within a hierarchy where each process can spawn multiple children, forming a tree structure. This not only clarifies the parent-child relationship but also provides insights into resource allocation and process allocation strategies. For example, a web server may handle connections by spawning child processes for each request, relieving the parent process of direct management and fostering a more efficient delegation of tasks.

In addition, processes exhibit various attributes that affect their behavior within the operating system. Resource usage characteristics —such as CPU time, memory consumption, and I/O operations— determine how effectively a process runs. The cumulative resource consumption across processes can affect system performance significantly. Thus, maintaining awareness of these characteristics is vital for troubleshooting and managing system health. Through proactive monitoring, administrators can identify processes that consume excessive resources, allowing for strategic pruning when necessary.

Lastly, considering system security and integrity, special attributes such as nice values and user permissions also impact process management. Nice values determine a process's execution priority, thereby influencing how much CPU time it receives relative to others. Understanding how to adjust these values is essential for managing resource contention, particularly in environments with multiple competing processes. Securing these processes through the right permissions elevates the responsibility of system administrators, ensuring that critical applications remain unimpeded by unauthorized interference.

In essence, the characteristics of processes in a Linux environment create a rich tapestry of interactions and relationships that require careful consideration. Mastering these elements equips administrators with the tools necessary to effectively monitor, optimize, and manage the complex processes that underpin system performance. Just as a bonsai artist carefully shapes and prunes their creation, so too must system administrators cultivate their Linux process tree, balancing efficiency, security, and stability in their operational practices. As we move forward in our exploration of Linux processes, a deeper understanding of these characteristics will lay the groundwork for more sophisticated manipulations and optimizations, ultimately enhancing the integrity and responsiveness of the system landscape.

2.3. Threads vs. Processes

In the intricate tapestry of Linux system management, understanding the distinction between threads and processes is paramount for optimizing performance and resource allocation. Though both threads and processes are fundamental to executing tasks in a computing environment, they represent different levels of granularity in multitasking—and their management comes with its own set of implications for performance, memory usage, and scalability.

At the most basic level, a process is defined as an instance of a running program. It acts as a sovereign entity that comes with its own allocated memory space, system resources, and security permissions. In contrast, a thread is a smaller unit of execution that exists within a process. A process can spawn multiple threads that share the same resources and memory space, but each thread operates independently to execute different parts of the program's logic. This intrinsic collaboration offers a potent mechanism for improving the efficiency of resource usage, especially in multi-core systems where threads can run concurrently, leveraging parallel processing capabilities.

The architecture of processes involves a clear separation of memory space. Each process encapsulates its code, data, stack, and heap, allowing it to operate in isolation from other processes. This isolation is essential for maintaining system stability and security, as each process has restricted access to the memory of others unless explicit inter-process communication (IPC) mechanisms are employed. This design minimizes the risk of one process inadvertently affecting the execution or data integrity of another, an essential aspect in a multi-user environment where processes could be running with varying degrees of permission and authority.

Conversely, threads within the same process share the same memory space, which allows for more efficient communication and reduced overhead. Since threads have access to the process's memory, they can exchange information more rapidly than if they were separate processes relying on IPC. However, this shared access introduces complexities such as synchronization issues. When multiple threads attempt to modify shared data, race conditions can occur, resulting in unpredictable behavior. Hence, robust synchronization mechanisms, like mutexes and semaphores, are indispensable in multi-threading to ensure data consistency and proper execution order.

Furthermore, the initiation of threads is less resource-intensive compared to processes. Creating a new thread generally requires fewer resources than spawning a full-fledged process. When a process creates a new thread, the operating system needs to allocate a smaller overhead for thread control structures and stack memory. In contrast, creating a new process involves allocating a separate memory space and duplicate resources, considerably increasing startup time and system overhead. Consequently, in high-performance applications such as web servers handling numerous connections or concurrent tasks, multithreading can significantly enhance responsiveness and throughput by allowing multiple tasks to run in tandem without the weight of full process creation overhead.

Performance also varies significantly between processes and threads in terms of scheduling and management. Operating systems generally use preemptive scheduling and maintain separate queues for processes and threads. Due to the lower overhead of context switching between threads compared to processes, threads can be scheduled more efficiently, allowing quicker handling of tasks. In scenarios where responsiveness is critical, such as interactive applications or real-time systems, multi-threading provides distinct advantages, allowing applications to remain responsive to user input while simultaneously processing background tasks.

However, this does not imply that threads are an unambiguous advantage. The shared memory space of threads necessitates careful consideration of design patterns to avoid pitfalls associated with concurrency. A poorly designed multi-threaded application may exhibit complex bugs that are hard to reproduce, as the timing of thread execution can significantly influence program behavior. Likewise, the management of threads often requires advanced fault tolerance strategies since a crash in one thread can compromise the entire process and consequently affect all threads within that process.

Security considerations also diverge between using processes and threads. Processes are inherently more secure due to their isolation; vulnerabilities or crashes in one process are unlikely to compromise others. In contrast, threads, while facilitating faster communication, share risks associated with the entire process's memory space. If one thread encounters an exception, it could bring down the entire process, complicating recovery. Therefore, deciding between using threads or processes might involve a trade-off between performance and risk management.

In terms of use cases, the choice between threads and processes is influenced heavily by the nature of the tasks at hand. Applications that prioritize parallel processing and can benefit from shared memory may prefer multithreading. Conversely, applications requiring robust isolation, fault tolerance, or subprocess management might lean towards using processes. For instance, web servers often utilize multiple threads to handle incoming requests rapidly, while complex data processing jobs (like those in scientific computing) may rely on separate processes for better data integrity and management.

In conclusion, threads and processes serve different purposes within the Linux system architecture, each with its advantages and drawbacks. Advanced system administrators must determine the most appropriate model based on specific workload demands, resource management strategies, and the need for isolation versus efficiency. A nuanced understanding of how both units operate vis-à-vis the overarching Linux process tree allows practitioners to architect responsive, efficient, and secure applications, ensuring that the operational landscape is as adaptable and resilient as a beautifully pruned bonsai. As you delve deeper into the intricacies of Linux processes, embracing the delicate balance between threads and processes will be essential in mastering process management in this dynamic environment.

2.4. The Process Lifecycle

Understanding the lifecycle of a process within a Linux operating system is vital for effective system administration. Just like the stages of life that a bonsai tree undergoes—germination, growth, pruning, and eventual rest—processes follow a distinct lifecycle that involves their creation, execution, and termination. Each phase is crucial for ensuring that resources are allocated efficiently and that each process performs its intended function within the system.

The process lifecycle begins at creation, which typically occurs when a program is initiated to run. In Linux, this is usually achieved through system calls like `fork()`, `exec()`, or `clone()`. When a program is invoked, the operating system reserves memory and allocates necessary resources for the process to execute. This initial phase not only involves creating a new process ID (PID) but also sets up the execution environment, including copying the process's initial state from its parent. During this state, the child process inherits attributes from its parent while possessing its own unique PID, creating a parent-child relationship that is vital for process management.

Execution follows creation. This is the phase where the process performs its intended tasks. As it executes, a process will move through various states defined by the operating system. Initially, it may enter the "running" state, actively using CPU resources to carry out instructions. During this phase, the scheduler plays a crucial role in determining which processes receive CPU time based on pre-defined priorities and scheduling algorithms. However, not all processes can run indefinitely; some may need to wait for resources, such as I/O operations, which triggers a transition to the "waiting" or "blocked" state. Processes may spend significant time in this state, especially if they rely on user input or external systems to continue executing.

The complexity of process execution is further underscored by the multi-threading capabilities of modern applications. Processes containing multiple threads allow for concurrent execution of tasks, but they must be carefully managed to avoid complications such as race conditions where threads compete for shared resources. Proper synchronization through mutexes or semaphores is essential in this phase to ensure that threads operate cohesively without conflict.

As a process continues to execute, its resources and status can evolve. It may transition to a "stopped" state if paused for debugging purposes or suspended by the system for various reasons, such as low system resources or administrative intervention. These various states —running, waiting, stopped—reflect how the process interacts with the system's resource manager and scheduler.

The termination of the process marks the final stage of its lifecycle. Once a process concludes its tasks, it must be correctly disposed of to reclaim the resources allocated to it. This is achieved through the exit process, where the process informs the system that it has completed its operations. After termination, the system will clear the memory space used by the process and release its PID, allowing for reuse by future processes. However, it's crucial to note that ungracefully terminated processes—those killed forcibly or crashing unexpectedly —can leave behind 'zombie' processes that occupy a PID without actual execution. These zombies can accumulate and reduce the total number of available PIDs, leading to operational issues unless properly monitored and cleaned up.

Throughout the entire lifecycle of a process, various system-level tools and commands can be employed to monitor, manage, and optimize processes. Commands like ps, top, and htop enable administrators to view current processes, analyze their states, and decide whether processes need to be terminated or adjusted based on their resource consumption. It's critical for systems administrators to regularly engage with these tools as they represent the primary means of interaction with the process lifecycle, ensuring that the Linux environment remains efficient and healthy.

Beyond just interaction with tools, understanding the lifecycle allows administrators to engage in proactive tuning of the process management system. By recognizing patterns of process behavior, seasoned administrators can identify often-repeated issues—whether they be resource bottlenecks or application crashes—and take appropriate steps to mitigate these problems in advance.

In conclusion, the lifecycle of a process within the Linux operating system encompasses a comprehensive spectrum of activities from creation through execution to termination. Each phase is interconnected, and understanding how to navigate each step effectively empowers administrators to maintain an agile, responsive system. Just as a bonsai artist trains their plant to thrive in harmony with its environment, so too must Linux system administrators shape their process trees to foster optimal application performance and overall system stability. Through the lens of this lifecycle, the art of managing processes becomes a more intricate, refined practice—ensuring that every process contributes meaningfully to the system's goal of efficient operation.

2.5. Inter-Process Communication

In Linux, processes are not isolated entities; rather, they engage in a continuous interplay with each other through various mechanisms of communication. This interplay is essential for effectively sharing data and coordinating activities across different processes, ensuring an efficient execution of tasks. Inter-Process Communication (IPC) refers to the techniques and tools that facilitate this exchange of information, and understanding them is critical for system administrators aiming to manage processes effectively and optimize system performance.

IPC mechanisms in Linux are diverse, each with unique characteristics that cater to different use cases and requirements. These mechanisms can generally be categorized into two main types: message-based and memory-based communication. Message-based IPC includes tools like message queues, pipes, and signals, while memory-based IPC is primarily represented by shared memory.

Message queues allow processes to send and receive messages in an organized manner, enabling processes to communicate without needing to be directly connected. This decoupling provides flexibility and can aid in building modular applications. A process can send a message to a queue, and another process can retrieve it at a later time, independent of the sender's state. This mechanism is especially useful when integrating asynchronous event-driven architectures into applications. The reliability of message queues ensures that messages are delivered in the order they were sent, allowing processes to synchronize their actions efficiently.

Pipes, on the other hand, are a simpler form of IPC, allowing one-way communication. A pipe can be used when the output of one process needs to be fed directly as the input to another. The data flows in a unidirectional stream from the writing process to the reading process, and it's commonly used in shell scripting and command chaining.

The inherent simplicity of pipes makes them a quick solution for data flow control, allowing for the construction of complex commands via simple concatenation.

Signals introduce another dimension to IPC by enabling asynchronous notification of events to processes. A signal acts like a software interrupt that informs a process of an event that requires immediate attention. For instance, the SIGKILL signal can instruct a process to terminate immediately. While powerful in their ability to coordinate actions at a high level, signals must be handled with care, as improper management can lead to resource leaks or deadlocks if a process fails to respond to a signal appropriately.

Shared memory, conversely, allows multiple processes to access the same block of memory, providing the fastest method for IPC due to its low overhead. However, this shared access necessitates stringent synchronization mechanisms to prevent race conditions and ensure data consistency. The use of semaphores, mutexes, and similar mechanisms becomes crucial in environments utilizing shared memory, as these tools manage access to ensure that only one process can write or read at a given time.

Understanding the various IPC mechanisms also involves recognizing their respective strengths and limitations. For example, message queues and pipes simplify the development process by abstracting the complications of managing shared memory, but they may introduce latency when processes need to send and receive frequent updates. On the other hand, while shared memory is faster, it requires careful handling and can complicate code, especially when multiple processes must synchronize their actions.

In environments where real-time processing is essential, the choice of IPC mechanism can dramatically impact system performance. For instance, multimedia applications, gaming servers, or other contexts requiring rapid response times may leverage shared memory to minimize delays. Conversely, systems designed for robust fault tolerance might favor message queues due to their reliability in ensuring messages are not lost in the event of process failure.

The Linux operating system provides various tools for managing IPC, including standard system calls like `msgget`, `msgsnd`, `msgrcv` for message queues, and `shmget`, `shmat`, `shmctl` for shared memory. Understanding these tools, their parameters, and their return codes is foundational for implementing effective IPC in any application. Furthermore, tools like `ipcs` and `ipcrm` allow administrators to view and manage existing IPC resources, making it easier to troubleshoot any issues or conflicts that might arise in an environment heavily reliant on IPC.

Moreover, the rise of modern application architectures, such as microservices and distributed systems, has further highlighted the need for effective and scalable IPC solutions. As Linux continues to underpin countless server environments, mastering IPC mechanisms will serve as a critical competency for system administrators, allowing them to build responsive and high-performing applications.

In conclusion, effective inter-process communication is the lifeblood of a well-functioning Linux system. It allows processes to collaborate, share data, and operate in harmony, optimizing the overall performance of applications. By understanding and harnessing the various IPC mechanisms available, administrators can not only enhance the efficiency of their applications but also proactively address potential bottlenecks and create a robust framework for process management. As we hone our skills in this area, we take another step toward perfecting the balance that keeps our Linux systems healthy and responsive—akin to the delicate art of bonsai pruning that ensures a flourishing tree.

3. Navigating the Process Tree

3.1. Parent and Child Processes

In the Linux operating system, the arrangement of processes embodies a well-structured hierarchy that can be visualized as a tree, with each process having a unique place within this configuration. This hierarchy consists of parent and child processes, where a parent process might create one or more child processes. Understanding this relationship is fundamental for system administrators as it influences resource management, system stability, and process control.

At the heart of the parent-child dynamic is the process creation mechanism, often initiated through system calls such as fork(). When a parent process invokes the fork() command, it generates a copy of itself—the child process. This child inherits certain attributes from its parent, including environment variables and memory space, but possesses its independent execution context marked by a distinct Process ID (PID). This separation is crucial as it allows the child process to execute tasks concurrently without interfering with the operation of the parent process.

The parent-child relationship fosters a collaborative approach within the Linux process model. The parent often delegates tasks to its children, which can improve overall system efficiency. For example, in a web server context, the parent process might listen for incoming connections and spawn child processes to handle each request. This model not only enhances responsiveness but also isolates tasks within their own processes, improving stability; if one child encounters an error or crashes, the parent can continue running and managing additional requests.

Moreover, parent processes can exercise control over their child processes through various management commands. System administrators can utilize commands such as kill to send signals that dictate the behavior of these processes. For instance, the parent might need to terminate a child that is consuming excessive resources or has gone awry. This level of control is critical in maintaining the overall health of the system. The relationship between parent and child processes thus aligns with broader resource management strategies, ensuring critical applications and services maintain their integrity.

The interaction between parent and child processes also extends to process monitoring and diagnostics. Tools like `ps` and `top` provide insights into how processes are interrelated within the tree structure. By examining the process tree, administrators can quickly ascertain which processes are child processes of a particular parent, allowing for more streamlined troubleshooting and optimization. This visibility is essential in environments where resource contention is a consistent concern, as it helps pinpoint processes that may be impeding performance.

Additionally, the hierarchical structure of processes facilitates a more organized approach to resource allocation and handling dependencies. When a parent process creates a child, it is implicitly signaling a dependency relationship where the parent often manages the life cycle of the child. Understanding these relationships aids administrators in implementing failover strategies and automating recovery processes should a child process terminate unexpectedly. Designing a structure that acknowledges these dependencies can lead to robust process management strategies that minimize downtime and enhance fault tolerance.

In the context of Linux, practices such as Zombie processes—child processes that have completed execution but have not been reaped by their parent—also illustrate the importance of managing parent-child relationships. If not monitored and handled properly, these processes can occupy valuable system resources and diminish performance over time. Tools such as `ps aux` and `top` become vital for identifying and addressing such issues.

Furthermore, the intricacies of process management evolve when considering multi-threaded applications. Here, the concept of parent and child processes expands to encompass threads within a single process, which can significantly affect performance and resource management. While each thread within a multi-threaded application shares the same memory and resources, their ability to operate independently can also complicate debugging and error tracing. The dynamic aspect of threading introduces additional considerations for system administrators when assessing the health and stability of their processes.

Through understanding the vital role of parent and child processes, administrators gain insights into the underlying architecture of their Linux systems. This knowledge not only guides effective resource allocation but enables more sophisticated monitoring and maintenance strategies. By mastering the parent-child process relationship, system administrators can ensure that their systems are responsive, stable, and optimized for the myriad tasks they are designed to handle.

In summary, the parent-child process relationship within the Linux process tree is an essential cornerstone of effective process management. It contributes to both the design and operational efficiency of applications running on Linux. As you explore further into process management, appreciating this hierarchy will enhance your capability to manage complexity and ensure system health, thereby allowing your Linux environment to flourish much like a meticulously cared-for bonsai tree, thriving with balance and beauty amidst the intricacies of its ecosystem. Through effective navigation of the process tree, you will cultivate a deeper understanding of the delicate interactions that sustain a well-functioning system, positioning yourself as a proficient steward in the realm of Linux administration.

3.2. Forking and Cloning

Forking and cloning are two fundamental mechanisms used in Linux system programming to create new processes, forming the backbone of multitasking and resource management in the operating system. Gaining insight into these processes is essential for understanding how applications execute concurrently and efficiently on a Linux system.

To begin, forking—a key aspect of process management—is executed through the `fork()` system call. This command enables a process, known as the parent process, to create a duplicate process, referred to as the child process. When a parent calls `fork()`, the operating system generates a new Process ID (PID) for the child, copies the parent's process state, and establishes a unique execution context for it. The child inherits various attributes from the parent, including its memory space, file descriptors, and environment variables, but runs as an independent entity that can execute commands, modify its state, and interact with other processes.

The `fork()` operation succeeds in the majority of scenarios and returns two values: for the parent, it returns the child's PID, while for the child, it returns 0. This unique return value allows both processes to identify their status within the system and dictate their subsequent actions. For instance, after forking, the parent process could proceed to perform its tasks or wait for the child to complete, while the child could execute a different block of code tailored to its purpose.

The use of forking is pervasive in server applications, where a parent process accepts incoming connections and spawns child processes to handle each one individually. This delegation significantly increases the responsiveness of applications as they can manage multiple requests simultaneously.

However, the memory model in Unix-like systems imposes challenges when it comes to efficiency. On creation, the child process initially shares pages with the parent (copy-on-write), meaning both share the same physical memory until one side modifies the shared resource. Once a modification happens, the operating system duplicates that page so each process can maintain its own copy. This optimization allows systems to conserve memory, especially in scenarios where processes are frequently forked without needing to change much initially.

Yet, for more specific use cases, a more sophisticated form of process creation exists: cloning. This is achieved through the `clone()` system call, which offers greater flexibility than fork(). While fork() creates a new process that inherits everything from the parent, clone() allows developers to specify exactly which resources are shared between the parent and child. This mechanism is utilized primarily for creating threads where multiple execution paths share parts of the parent's memory space.

The clone() function's versatility comes from its ability to define flags that control the shared resources, such as memory and processing resources. For instance, it can create a child process that shares its memory space with the parent while isolating other resources, like file descriptors and execution state. This finely grained control over resource sharing is particularly advantageous in threaded programming, as it minimizes overhead and maximizes communication speed between threads.

Moreover, clone() can be configured to implement robust process models that cater to various operating system needs, including lightweight threading models used in modern applications. In a Linux environment, both fork() and clone() play pivotal roles in managing concurrency, where efficient utilization of processes and threads can directly affect system performance and application responsiveness.

While both mechanisms are crucial for process management, their application depends on the specific needs of the application. Forking is typically preferred for creating isolated processes that require independent execution, while cloning is favored for building highly concurrent applications or in instances where shared memory space is beneficial.

In conclusion, understanding forking and cloning serves as a cornerstone for mastering Linux process management. These mechanisms determine how processes interact, share resources, and perform tasks concurrently within the Linux operating system. As system administrators, developers, or anyone involved with Linux systems, grasping these concepts enriches your ability to manage processes effectively and optimize application performance—you bring the fine art of system management to life, sculpting the process tree with an understanding that echoes the meticulous attentiveness of a bonsai master pruning and nurturing their trees to flourish. Embracing forking and cloning as two powerful tools can lead to innovative application designs and optimizations, making you adept in the art of Linux process control at a fundamental level.

3.3. Process Identification and Naming

When managing processes in a Linux environment, understanding how to effectively identify and name them is fundamental. Every process is not just a unit of execution; it embodies a conceptual identity that forms part of a more extensive ecosystem. By mastering process identification and naming conventions, system administrators can navigate the complex tree of processes with precision and ease, making informed decisions that enhance the performance and stability of the Linux system.

A process is characterized by two primary identifiers: the Process ID (PID) and the Process name. The PID is a unique numeric identifier assigned by the operating system that distinguishes one process from another. As processes are created and terminated, the kernel manages these identifiers dynamically, reusing PIDs from processes that have exited. However, administrators need to recognize that PIDs are only temporary labels; they are assigned and reassigned as the system evolves. This means that a PID's value can change over time, but its role as an identifier within the currently active process entries in the process table remains critical.

The naming of processes operates concurrently with PIDs, serving as a human-readable string that describes what the process does. A well-chosen process name can provide clarity regarding the function of each process, which is especially valuable in environments where numerous processes run concurrently. For example, a process executing an Apache web server might be named httpd, while a database management system might be running under the name mysqld. These designations not only aid in human recognition but also assist in automated monitoring tools that filter and report based on process names.

One common tool for identifying processes is the ps command, which displays a snapshot of current processes. By executing ps aux, you receive a detailed list that includes user ownership, PID, CPU and memory utilization, and the command that initiated the process. The various columns in this output provide essential context; for instance, processes with high CPU and memory utilization may require further investigation or may need to be terminated to maintain system performance. Knowing how to filter this data—either by user, PID, or associated command—enables administrators to quickly locate and manage specific tasks within the intricate process tree.

Another valuable command is top, which provides a real-time, interactive view of running processes. The top display updates continuously and allows users to sort and filter processes based on multiple criteria, such as CPU usage, memory usage, or even the next scheduled execution time. This dynamic nature is particularly important for system administrators who need to monitor performance and react swiftly to any signs of process-related issues. The ability to see which processes are consuming system resources enables targeted intervention, preventing resource contention and ensuring system health.

Advanced process management might also involve using textual representations of processes in scripts and automation tools. For example, when you need to kill a specific process without manually looking it up in interactive commands, employing a command like kill $(pidof process_name) allows for seamless termination based on the naming of the process. Here, pidof retrieves the PID of the named process dynamically, showcasing how naming conventions can streamline administration tasks.

In scripting, consistently used naming conventions play a role in process identification as well. For example, it's common practice to name processes in a predictable manner, which facilitates maintenance and troubleshooting. This practice can lead to standardized naming schemes within an organization, improving communication amongst team members and contributing to more effective system management.

Moreover, specialized tools for process monitoring, like `htop`, offer enhanced features compared to traditional alternatives. They not only display the process name and PID but also provide an interactive interface for easy navigation and management of system resources. Named processes are often color-coded based on their resource usage, which helps in quickly identifying processes that might need immediate attention.

In addition to identifying and naming processes, it is also vital to understand how hierarchical naming structures work within the context of parent-child relationships. A graphical representation of processes as a tree shows the relationships between parent process IDs (PPID) and their corresponding child processes; visualizing this hierarchy can clarify how tasks are distributed and managed within the system. There are several commands like `pstree` that illustrate this relationship comprehensively, offering an overview of process dependencies, which assists administrators in making informed decisions about restarting, killing, or prioritizing processes.

In conclusion, process identification and naming are foundational elements of effective Linux process management. By utilizing unique PIDs, clear naming conventions, and a range of command-line tools, administrators can maintain a sharp focus on their system's operations. The interplay between PIDs and process names not only enhances manual management but also streamlines automation and scripting efforts. Just as a bonsai artist identifies and nurtures each branch within their carefully cultivated tree, adept system administrators must engage with each process to prevent overgrowth, ensuring that the Linux process tree remains balanced, responsive, and healthy. Mastery in process identification and naming enables administrators to prune the cascading roots of processes efficiently, cultivating an agile and robust Linux environment.

3.4. Role of init and Systemd

The Linux operating system has evolved considerably since its inception, with process management emerging as a fundamental component of its architecture. Central to this process management is the role of the init system, which serves as the first process to run at boot time and as the parent of all other processes in the system. Traditionally, Unix-like systems utilized the original init system, which followed a simple, linear approach to initializing the system services and processes. However, as system requirements grew more complex and diverse, the limitations of traditional init systems became evident, leading to the development and widespread adoption of systemd.

Systemd is a modern init system that offers a more efficient and flexible approach to process management. Its primary function is to boot the system and manage its services, but the breadth of its responsibilities extends far beyond these basic requirements. Systemd handles service dependencies, parallelizes service startup, and offers advanced features such as socket activation and on-demand service start-up. This enhanced capability allows for faster boot times and more responsive system performance, which is essential in today's environments where users demand efficient, quick access to services.

Understanding the role of init and systemd in process management reveals the intricate interplay between system processes. When a Linux system boots up, the kernel loads and executes the init process. Init, assigned the Process ID (PID) of 1, serves as the parent for all subsequent processes. It reads its configuration files, initializing various services based on the specified targets in the system.

In contrast, the transition to systemd represents a paradigm shift that brings with it a new set of responsibilities and design philosophies. A key feature of systemd is its use of "units," which are standardized configuration files that define how a given process is managed. There are several types of units, including service units, socket units, mount units, and timer units. This modular approach allows administrators more granular control over process management, enabling them to start, stop, and configure services independently, tailoring the system to specific needs.

The introduction of service dependencies into systemd adds another layer of sophistication in process management. Systemd tracks dependencies between services, ensuring that services are started in the correct order based on their requirements. For instance, a web server may depend on a database service being operational before it can start. If the database service fails to launch, systemd will know to prevent the web server from starting, thereby avoiding potential errors. This capacity for intelligent service management is a significant improvement over traditional init systems, which often followed a less nuanced start-up sequence.

Moreover, systemd also embraces parallelization, allowing multiple services to start concurrently, significantly reducing boot time and enhancing overall performance. By examining the dependencies and employing sockets for activation, systemd can launch services only when required, rather than starting everything at boot with the potential of unnecessary resource consumption. This feature is particularly useful in servers and embedded systems, where optimizing resource usage is critical to performance.

Another distinct aspect of systemd is its logging capabilities, integrated through the journal system, which collects logs from all activated services in a unified manner. This provides system administrators with rich diagnostic information that aids in troubleshooting and monitoring service behavior. The availability of detailed logs linked to specific services allows administrators to quickly identify what went wrong during a service startup or during execution over time. Logs can be queried conveniently with tools such as journalctl, allowing for efficient retrieval of relevant log entries based on service units or time frames.

The interaction between init (and systemd) and process management doesn't stop at boot time; it continues through the lifecycle of every process within the Linux environment. Both systems allow for process tracking, with commands like `systemctl` enabling administrators to manage active processes, check their statuses, and control their execution. For example, using systemd, one can easily stop a service and restart it, view logs, enable or disable services from starting at boot, and monitor the overall health of system services.

In summary, the role of init and systemd in process management is pivotal in the Linux ecosystem. They provide a robust framework for not only booting the system and starting critical services but also managing the numerous processes that run on it. Through improved dependency management, parallel service initialization, detailed logging mechanisms, and a modular unit-based system, systemd redefines how administrators approach process management, offering tools that enhance both the performance and reliability of Linux-based environments. As we further explore the complexities of process management in Linux, the relationship between systemd, processes, and the overall system architecture will offer deeper insights into crafting an optimal operating system experience, much like the nuanced care required in pruning a bonsai tree to achieve its ideal form.

3.5. Process Priorities and Scheduling

In any operating system, the management of processes is a crucial component that directly affects performance, responsiveness, and resource distribution. This area is particularly vital in Linux systems where multiple processes can simultaneously execute tasks, creating a robust environment that requires careful orchestration. One of the key aspects that underpin effective process management is the concept of process priorities and scheduling. Understanding how priorities influence the execution order of processes is essential for optimizing system performance and ensuring that critical tasks receive the attention they require.

At its core, the priority of a process dictates how the Linux kernel schedules it in relation to other running processes. Linux employs a priority-based scheduling algorithm where each process is assigned a unique priority level. The scheduling system utilizes this priority to determine which processes are granted CPU time and how much time they receive. In most scenarios, processes with higher priority values are favored over those with lower values, meaning they will be executed first or given greater access to resources when contention arises.

In Linux, process priorities can generally be categorized into two types: real-time priorities and time-sharing priorities. Real-time priorities, which range from 1 to 99, are used for processes that require immediate attention, ensuring lower latency for operations that are time-sensitive—like audio processing or real-time gaming. Conversely, time-sharing priorities range from 100 to 139 and are designed for tasks that can tolerate more latency—such as desktop applications or background services. The dynamic adjustment of these priorities allows the operating system to emphasize tasks based on their urgency and resource requirements.

Moreover, the system administrator has the ability to adjust the priorities of processes using the `nice` and `renice` commands. The `nice` command is used at launch to set a specific priority for a new process, while `renice` can modify the priority of an already running process. A crucial aspect of using these commands effectively lies in understanding their numerical values—lower nice values correspond to higher actual scheduling priority. For instance, issuing a command like `nice -n -5 myProcess` would elevate the priority of `myProcess`, allowing it to execute with more urgency than other processes with default nice values.

The scheduling policies in Linux are what ultimately harmonize the interplay between priorities and execution. The Completely Fair Scheduler (CFS), which is the default process scheduler in many Linux kernel versions, aims to allocate CPU time equitably among processes while adhering to their assigned priorities. CFS uses a fair time-slice allocation strategy where it keeps track of how much CPU time each process has consumed and ensures that no single process monopolizes system resources. This fair approach allows high-priority tasks to respond more quickly without starving lower-priority processes entirely.

In addition to CFS, real-time processes are managed by the Real-Time Scheduler. This specialized scheduler handles real-time tasks according to their priorities, guaranteeing them response times suitable for applications that require precision and minimal latency. It implements FIFO (First In, First Out) scheduling alongside round-robin techniques for time-sliced real-time processes—ensuring that high-priority processes receive immediate CPU access while preventing starvation of lower-priority ones.

Understanding how to manipulate process priorities and scheduling effectively requires familiarity with monitoring tools available in Linux. The top and htop commands play significant roles in this aspect—both displaying real-time information about running processes, including their current priority levels and CPU usage. Administrators can quickly assess which processes may need to have their priorities adjusted to ensure critical operations maintain their performance levels.

When administrators delve into performance tuning, especially in environments with heavy workloads or critical applications, the ability to adjust process priorities becomes a powerful tool for achieving optimal results. For instance, if an application managing user sessions in a web server environment starts to lag due to excessive CPU load, an administrator might lower the priority of less important background processes to alleviate the strain. Simultaneously, they may choose to elevate the priority of the affected application, ensuring it receives the resources required to perform effectively.

However, with great power comes great responsibility. It is vital to apply these changes judiciously, as setting priorities incorrectly can lead to adverse effects. For instance, excessively elevating a process's priority could starve others, causing them to respond slowly or even halt. Additionally, improper management of real-time processes can result in system instability and unresponsive states, particularly if too many processes are vying for real-time scheduling.

Furthermore, another critical factor to consider regarding priorities and scheduling is how they impact system resource allocation, especially in multi-core environments. Effective load balancing through priority management ensures that processing cores are utilized efficiently, preventing bottlenecks and ensuring smooth operation across the system. Administrators must be adept in analyzing resource distribution through tools and metrics to make educated decisions regarding process prioritization.

In conclusion, mastering process priorities and scheduling within the Linux operating system is critical for achieving a responsive and efficient environment. By understanding the roles of real-time and time-sharing priorities, leveraging monitoring tools, and judiciously adjusting process priorities, administrators can sculpt their systems to optimize performance. As with the art of bonsai, the practice of process management requires careful consideration and a steady hand; with focus and diligence, one can promote a harmonious balance that flourishes in the complex landscape of Linux processes.

4. Mastering the 'Top' Command

4.1. Installing and Configuring 'Top'

To set up the 'Top' command on your Linux system, you need to understand that 'Top' is generally included by default in most Linux distributions. As a command-line utility, it provides a dynamic, real-time view of active processes on the system, allowing you to keep tabs on system resource usage and performance. While it typically does not require a separate installation, you may need to install the package in some distributions where it may not be included by default, especially in minimalist setups.

Start by verifying if 'Top' is already installed on your system. You can do this by opening a terminal window and typing:

top

If the command executes and shows you the process list, then 'Top' is installed correctly. If you receive an error indicating that the command is not found, you will need to install it.

To install 'Top', you can use your distribution's package manager:

• On Debian-based systems (like Ubuntu), you would use:

sudo apt update sudo apt install procps

• For Red Hat-based systems (like CentOS or Fedora), the command would be:

sudo yum install procps-ng

• For Arch Linux, you could use:

sudo pacman -S procps-ng

Once installed, you can start using 'Top' right away by typing top into your terminal.

Now, moving on to configuring 'Top', while the default settings are quite functional, there are several configuration options available that can enhance your experience and allow you to tailor the display to your needs. You can interact with 'Top' using keyboard commands, which allows you to sort, filter, and modify what is displayed in real-time.

To enter setup mode in 'Top', you can press the Z command, which opens the setup menu. In this menu, you will find options that let you toggle various display settings such as which columns to show, the order of the processes listed, and the format of the output. For instance, you can enable or disable specific columns like memory usage (%MEM), process ID (PID), user ID (USER), and many others based on your monitoring requirements.

One of the fundamental settings you may want to adjust is the refresh interval. The default is set to 3 seconds, but this can be changed by pressing the 'd' key and specifying your desired delay in seconds.

To preserve your configurations, 'Top' often allows you to save your settings in a configuration file, which can lead to a consistent output format every time you run the utility. This file is usually called .toprc, and it is located in your home directory.

Additionally, if you're looking for a more persistent configuration, you can modify the configuration file directly or use the -p option when launching 'Top' to monitor specific process IDs by starting 'Top' with command:

top -p

This allows you to focus on specific processes without the distraction of other system tasks.

As you use 'Top', ongoing monitoring is essential to ensure your Linux system runs efficiently and resources are allocated effectively. With its real-time capabilities and extensive customization options, mastering 'Top' can significantly enhance your process management strategy. Whether you are diagnosing system bottlenecks, identifying resource hogs, or simply monitoring background tasks, 'Top' serves as a powerful ally in your quest for a responsive and efficient Linux environment. By articulating your configuration and understanding its core functions, you're well on your way to harnessing its full potential to prune your system's process tree effectively.

4.2. Reading Top's Display

To effectively navigate and utilize the 'Top' command on your Linux system, it is essential to understand its display, which presents a wealth of information about the current state of running processes. The format and organization of this display are designed to provide users with a comprehensive overview of system performance, resource allocation, and process activity, enabling informed decisions about process management.

Upon launching 'Top', you are greeted with two main sections: the summary area at the top and the task area below it. Each of these sections presents critical information that can influence how you interact with the system.

Starting with the summary area, it includes key system metrics that provide an immediate understanding of overall system health. The elements typically displayed include:

1. System Uptime: This indicates how long the system has been running since the last boot. It is often presented in a format that shows days, hours, and minutes, providing a quick snapshot of system stability.

2. Load Average: Displayed as three numerical values representing the average system load over the last 1, 5, and 15 minutes. Understanding load averages is crucial, as they indicate how many processes are actively competing for CPU time. A high load average compared to the number of CPU cores could signal potential performance issues.

3. Number of Tasks: This provides a count of all processes on the system, separated by their state, such as running, sleeping, stopped, or zombie processes. This breakdown assists in understanding the overall process management landscape.

4. CPU Usage: This section details how CPU resources are being utilized. It typically breaks down CPU usage into various categories, such as user, system, idle, and nice (background processes). Familiarity with these metrics allows administrators to identify processes consuming excessive CPU resources quickly.

5. Memory Usage: Similar to CPU usage, this area presents information regarding the RAM and swap space utilization. This includes total memory, used memory, free memory, buffers, and cache. Tracking memory metrics helps ensure that the system isn't running low on resources, which could affect performance.

6. Swap Usage: This indicates how much swap space is in use. Excessive reliance on swap can slow down system performance, as accessing stored data from swap is significantly slower than from RAM.

Next is the task area, which lists individual processes, providing detailed information about each one. The columns typically displayed in this section include:

1. PID (Process ID): A unique identifier assigned to each running process, crucial for managing and controlling process behavior.

2. USER: The owner of the process, which can aid in identifying processes that should be managed based on user privileges.

3. PR (Priority): Indicates the scheduling priority of the process. A lower numerical value corresponds to a higher priority, guiding CPU scheduling.

4. NI (Nice Value): This represents the "nice" value used to alter the priority of the process; it can range from −20 (highest priority) to 19 (lowest priority).

5. VIRT: Shows the virtual memory size allocated for the process, including all code, data, and shared libraries.

6. RES: Reveals the resident memory size, which indicates the physical memory currently occupied by the process.

7. SHR: This reflects the amount of shared memory utilized, offering insights into how resources are being shared among processes.

8. S (State): Displays the current state of the process, such as S (sleeping), R (running), Z (zombie), or other states. Understanding these statuses is essential for effectively managing resources and identifying idle processes.

9. %CPU: The percentage of CPU time consumed by the process over the last sampling period, critical for performance management.

10. %MEM: Indicates the percentage of RAM used by the process, allowing for quick assessment of memory usage.

11. TIME+: Represents the total CPU time consumed by the process since it started, useful for evaluating long-running processes.

12. COMMAND: The command name or command line that initiated the process, providing context for what each process does.

Engaging with these metrics allows administrators to prioritize and manage processes based on their needs effectively. For instance, a strategic approach to monitoring running processes through 'Top' might involve focusing on processes consuming excess CPU or memory resources, thereby facilitating adjustments to regain system responsiveness.

Interactivity is one of the powerful features of 'Top', allowing real-time management of processes directly from the interface. Users can sort processes by various columns (such as memory or CPU usage), filter specific tasks, or send commands to alter processes without exiting the tool. For example, pressing 'k' allows you to kill a selected process directly by entering its PID, while 'r' can be used to change a process's nice value to adjust its priority.

In conclusion, reading 'Top's display effectively requires familiarity with its structure and the significance of the information presented. Mastering these elements not only enhances your ability to monitor system performance but also empowers you to manage processes dynamically, fostering an optimized and responsive Linux environment. Just as a bonsai artist learns to read the tree's needs through its shape and growth, so too must you become attuned to the signals your system presents, shaping a well-maintained process landscape through insightful management practices. By harnessing the full capabilities of 'Top', you position yourself as a knowledgeable steward of your Linux system, capable of pruning and nurturing processes with expertise.

4.3. Interactive Commands and Usage

Understanding interactive commands and their usage within the 'Top' command in Linux is pivotal for system administrators aiming to optimize their workflow and enhance process management efficiency. The interactive nature of 'Top' allows users to manipulate and control aspects of process monitoring directly from the console, offering a dynamic and flexible approach to assessing the health of a system in real-time.

Upon launching 'Top', you will notice an interface that continuously updates, providing a wealth of information about system performance and active processes. However, the real power of 'Top' comes from its array of interactive commands, which can be used to sort, manage, and customize the display according to your monitoring needs. Understanding these commands can significantly increase your efficiency in managing processes and diagnosing system issues.

One of the first commands you'll want to master is the ability to change the sorting order of the displayed processes. By default, 'Top' sorts processes by CPU usage, providing immediate insight into which processes are consuming the most resources. To adjust this sorting, simply press the 'O' key, which will prompt you to select the field by which to sort. You can sort by various metrics such as memory usage, process ID (PID), and more, depending on your needs. This flexible sorting mechanism allows administrators to focus on the most critical processes impacting system performance at any given moment.

Additionally, filtering processes is another crucial component of interactive commands in 'Top'. By pressing the 'u' key, you can specify a particular user whose processes you wish to monitor. This filtering capability becomes essential in multi-user environments where separating the processes of different users can clarify resource usage and assist in troubleshooting. It's particularly beneficial when diagnosing issues for specific users or services, allowing you to quickly isolate and address potential problems.

Another cornerstone of efficient process management in 'Top' is the ability to send signals to processes. By selecting a process and pressing the 'k' key, you can initiate a command to kill that process. The system will prompt you for the PID of the process you wish to terminate and the signal you want to send. The default signal is SIGTERM (15), which requests a graceful shutdown of the process, but you can opt for SIGKILL (9) to terminate it immediately. This functionality allows for quick intervention when a process is hogging resources or behaving erratically, empowering administrators to maintain system stability actively.

The refresh rate of the 'Top' interface is another interactive element that administrators should leverage. By pressing the 'd' key, you can adjust the update interval for the display, allowing you to speed up or slow down the refresh rate based on how frequently you need current information. A shorter interval provides a more dynamic view, while a longer interval can help minimize distraction and allow for focused analysis.

Another useful command is the ability to toggle the display of additional columns. By pressing the 'Z' key, users can open the setup menu, which allows for adding or removing various columns to the display based on preference. You can choose to show information such as the nice value (NI), command line arguments (COMMAND), and more. This customization allows you to tailor the output to match your administrative needs, focusing on relevant data that aids in your monitoring and troubleshooting efforts.

If you find the need to change the process priority during runtime, 'Top' allows for that too. By pressing the 'r' key and entering the desired PID, you can modify the nice value of any process on the fly, temporarily elevating or lowering its priority. This adjustment can be particularly useful when balancing resource allocation among competing processes.

Moreover, the interactive nature of 'Top' does not stop at process management; it also plays a vital role in monitoring system health comprehensively. Real-time data about memory usage, system load averages, and individual process characteristics keep you informed about the overall performance of your environment. Observing these patterns can alert you to potential problems before they grow, such as recognizing when memory usage approaches critical levels, indicating a need for further action or investigation.

For visual learners, understanding and navigating the 'Top' interface can be enhanced through the use of color-coded outputs found in many configurations of 'Top'. Bright colors often indicate differing usage levels, helping administrators quickly parse through the data displayed on the console. It is advisable to familiarize yourself with this color scheme during your ongoing interactions, as it can help indicate system abnormalities at a glance.

Lastly, ensuring your 'Top' command retains its configuration and custom settings across sessions is an interactive feature not to be overlooked. By saving your setup in the .toprc file, you ensure that every time 'Top' is launched, it reflects your desired columns and display options, saving time and maintaining consistency in monitoring approaches.

In conclusion, mastering the interactive commands and usage within the 'Top' command not only empowers you to monitor and manage processes effectively, but it also cultivates a proactive stance toward maintaining system efficiency and stability. By employing these commands skillfully, you fine-tune your monitoring capabilities, allowing for swift diagnostics and real-time interventions in a Linux environment. Much like a finely honed bonsai tool, your command over 'Top' equips you to prune and shape the process tree, ensuring it flourishes with the balance and health required for optimal performance. Through persistent practice and exploration of these interactive commands, you become adept in the intricate dance of Linux process management.

4.4. Sorting and Filtering Process Information

In managing processes using 'Top', sorting and filtering the displayed process information constitutes an essential capability that can significantly enhance your efficiency in monitoring and optimizing resource allocation on a Linux system. Mastering these functions allows you to prioritize the most critical processes, identify resource-heavy applications, and streamline your administrative tasks effectively.

When you launch 'Top', it presents a live view of all running processes, but without sorting and filtering, the sheer volume of information can become overwhelming. The default sorting criterion in 'Top' is CPU usage, meaning the processes consuming the most CPU resources are displayed at the top. However, as a system administrator, your needs go beyond simply identifying high CPU usage. Sorting and filtering functionalities enable you to access precisely the information you need quickly and intuitively.

To sort process information in 'Top', you utilize various keyboard commands that trigger immediate changes in the display. Pressing 'M' sorts the processes based on memory usage percentage, which is particularly useful if you suspect that memory bloat is affecting system performance. By pressing 'P', you return to sorting by CPU usage. Each time you execute these commands, you can instantly see the processes that require the most system resources, enabling you to make more informed decisions about where to focus your attention.

Additionally, 'Top' allows you to sort processes in a customized manner beyond the default fields. Pressing 'O' opens the sort order menu, where you can select different criteria such as PID (Process ID), user, or other metrics like nice value or time. This capability allows you to tailor the process information display to suit your monitoring goals. For instance, if you want to investigate processes initiated by a specific user, sorting by user will yield an immediate overview of those processes, facilitating targeted management.

Filtering processes based on user or command is an equally critical aspect of managing process data in 'Top'. By pressing 'u', you can enter a specific username to filter and display only the processes associated with that user. This filtering feature is particularly vital in multi-user environments where isolating a user's processes can clarify resource consumption and facilitate troubleshooting without the noise of irrelevant processes.

Another filtering technique involves utilizing the 'f' key to configure the displayed columns. Once in this setup mode, you can exclude non-essential columns from the interface, streamlining the display and retaining only the critical information you need to monitor effectively. This reduces clutter and enhances your ability to analyze data at a glance.

Additionally, you can use the command line options directly when launching 'Top' to focus on specific processes right from the outset. For example, executing `-p <PID>` lets you observe a particular process without distraction from others, providing a focused analysis space.

Moreover, interacting with the filtering options allows for dynamic engagement with process management. By combining sorting and filtering, you can monitor memory-intensive applications during a system strain more effectively. Should you identify a process that consistently consumes excessive memory or CPU, you can flag it for comprehensive investigation or take immediate action by terminating or adjusting its priority.

Another key feature is the capability to change the refresh interval at which 'Top' updates its displays. Pressing 'd' allows you to specify how often 'Top' should refresh its view, depending on your requirements. For instance, a faster refresh rate can provide real-time monitoring during critical evaluations but might be unnecessary during routine checks. Adjusting this setting enhances your ability to manage system performance fluidly.

As you become proficient in sorting and filtering process information in 'Top', your ability to maintain optimal system performance improves significantly. Whether it's managing resource-hogging applications or responding to active process demands, these tools empower you to navigate the complex landscape of Linux processes adeptly.

In conclusion, mastering sorting and filtering functionalities in 'Top' transforms a simple command-line utility into a potent tool for system performance management. You cultivate an environment where informed, timely decisions can be made, leading to improved system responsiveness and stability. By leveraging these capabilities to their fullest, you embrace the art of process management, ensuring that your Linux environment operates efficiently—much like a carefully pruned bonsai, thriving in its intentional and well-nurtured space.

4.5. Advanced Configuration Options

Advanced configuration options in the 'Top' command can dramatically enhance your ability to monitor processes effectively, tailoring the display to meet your specific needs and preferences. While the basic functionality of 'Top' provides a robust snapshot of performance metrics and processes in real-time, delving into its advanced settings allows for a more customized and efficient monitoring experience. We will explore some of these advanced configurations, focusing on both the adjustments available within the interactive interface and the ways to persistently modify settings for future sessions.

Starting with the interactive capabilities of 'Top', it's important to understand how to access the setup menu, which serves as the gateway to configuration options. You can enter the setup mode by pressing the 'Z' key while in 'Top'. This brings up the configuration screen where you can make a variety of adjustments to how process information is displayed.

Here, you can toggle various display options available in the columns listing processes. For instance, you might want to enable or disable certain metrics like %CPU, %MEM, TIME+, and others depending on your focus. If a particular metric does not inform your decision-making or if it clutters the display, removing it can provide a more streamlined view that highlights what is most relevant to you.

Another essential option available in the setup menu is changing the sort order of processes. By default, 'Top' typically sorts processes based on CPU usage; however, in the setup, you can specify an alternative sorting preference. For example, if your priority shifts towards memory-intensive processes, you could switch the sort order to memory usage. This enables you to quickly identify which processes are consuming significant amounts of RAM, which is critical data when managing system resources.

The refresh rate of the 'Top' display can also be adjusted, allowing you to control how frequently the information is updated. As previously mentioned, pressing the 'd' key during the session enables you to specify a new delay interval in seconds for refreshing the screen. Adjusting this setting can be particularly beneficial when you want to reduce distractions from constant updates or when you need more time to analyze certain processes without interruption.

For users who frequently monitor specific processes, you can save your configuration settings for future sessions. This is done by writing your preferences to the .toprc file in your home directory. When saving configurations, remember to test them out during your session; adjusting items like which columns are displayed and their order can drastically enhance your monitoring workflow. To persist settings, ensure to exit 'Top' properly to store these preferences.

Moreover, for administrators who work with multiple users on a system, filtering processes by user can be particularly useful. By pressing 'u' and entering a username, you can filter out processes that belong solely to that user. This functionality helps manage resource allocation effectively and provides clarity when troubleshooting specific user issues, streamlining the analysis process.

You can also monitor specific processes by using the -p option when launching the 'Top' command. For instance, executing top -p <PID> allows you to hone in on the performance of a particular process of interest right from the start, without sifting through a larger list. This targeted approach can be particularly advantageous during incident response situations, where the granular focus is needed.

Moreover, interactive signals through 'Top' enable real-time process control. For example, after selecting a process, pressing 'k' allows you to terminate it promptly, enhancing your ability to manage processes that may be causing issues with resource consumption or system performance directly from the interface. Likewise, if you need to change the nice value of a process, you can do so by selecting the process and pressing 'r'; this alteration adjusts the priority with which the process is treated by the system.

As you delve deeper into 'Top's advanced configurations, consider extending your process management capabilities by learning about additional command-line options. For instance, combining 'Top' with other command-line utilities in scripts or automated monitoring frameworks can extend its utility to broaden your process management toolkit.

In conclusion, mastering the advanced configuration options within the 'Top' command elevates your ability to monitor and manage processes in Linux significantly. By leveraging filtering, sorting, and displaying specific metrics suited to your needs, you transform 'Top' into a valuable resource for day-to-day system administration. Such mastery not only reflects an understanding of the tools at your disposal but also enables you to sculpt a process environment that thrives in efficiency and performance—akin to the artistry found in bonsai cultivation, where careful attention yields magnificent results. By continually engaging with these configurations, you position yourself optimally in your role, dedicating your efforts to cultivating a well-balanced and responsive system.

5. Exploring Alternative Tools

5.1. Using 'htop' for Enhanced Interaction

Using 'htop' for Enhanced Interaction

When it comes to process management on Linux systems, 'htop' stands out as an exceptional alternative to the traditional 'top' command. While 'top' provides essential insights into system performance through a command-line interface, 'htop' elevates user experience with a more intuitive and visually appealing presentation, making it a user-friendly upgrade for administrators and system users alike.

At its core, 'htop' is an interactive process viewer designed to display system processes and resource consumption in a more human-readable format. By utilizing a rich graphical interface, it allows users to navigate the process landscape with ease, highlighting key performance metrics and system resources in a way that encourages more efficient monitoring and management.

One of the most notable features of 'htop' is its colorful display, which visually distinguishes between various types of processes and resource usages. As you open 'htop', you are greeted by a series of colorful bars that represent the CPU, memory, and swap usage in real-time. This visual representation enables system administrators to grasp at a glance whether the server is under heavy load or running smoothly. Each colored bar corresponds to different aspects of system performance, making it straightforward to interpret the health of the system without sifting through lines of numerical data.

'htop' enhances interactivity substantially compared to 'top.' With just a few keystrokes, you can change the way you view processes, sort them according to various metrics, and perform actions. For instance, pressing function keys such as F6 allows you to choose how to sort your processes—be it by CPU usage, memory usage, or even time. This flexibility enables you to focus on the metrics most relevant to your current needs.

In addition to sorting, 'htop' also provides filtering options that can be accessed by pressing the F3 key. This allows users to quickly narrow down the list of processes based on specific criteria, such as name or user. Filtering is especially useful in environments running numerous processes, as it helps identify particular applications or services that require attention without being overwhelmed by data.

One of 'htop's standout features is its ability to manage processes directly from the interface. By selecting a process and pressing F9, users can kill or send various signals to processes. This capability effectively combines monitoring and management in one interface, enabling administrators to respond swiftly to any issues without switching between different command-line tools or utilities. The inclusion of signal options when terminating a process allows for graceful shutdowns, ensuring that applications can clean up resources as needed.

'htop' facilitates customization in several ways. Users can modify their display preferences, such as changing the columns shown, adjusting the refresh rate for real-time updates, and even altering the color scheme to suit personal preferences or to improve visibility under different terminal themes. These customizable settings help enhance user experience and can be tailored to align with specific monitoring tasks.

Another key feature of 'htop' is the capability to display processes in a tree view, which can be accessed by pressing F5. This hierarchical representation reveals the parent-child relationships between processes, making it easy to visualize how resources are allocated and which processes are dependent on others. Understanding these relationships is crucial for troubleshooting and performance optimization, as it highlights process dependencies that could impact system health.

As you dive deeper into using 'htop,' you'll find additional features such as process renicing, which allows you to adjust a process's priority without needing to exit the interface. By selecting a process and pressing F7 or F8, you can increase or decrease its nice value, respectively. This real-time capability is invaluable for managing resource contention dynamically as demands change.

Moreover, 'htop' supports setup options by pressing F2. This option opens a configuration menu, letting you customize various aspects of the program, such as defining which metrics to display and how they should be arranged. You can enable or disable specific columns, set up filters, or even choose to show additional information like the command line used to start a process.

Installing 'htop' is typically straightforward on most Linux distributions. You can generally find it in your package manager, and installation is as simple as running commands such as 'sudo apt install htop' on Debian-based systems or 'sudo yum install htop' on Red Hat-based systems. Once installed, you can launch 'htop' by typing simply 'htop' into your terminal, immediately accessing an enhanced view of your system's processes.

In conclusion, 'htop' represents a significant advancement in process management tools for Linux. Its interactive features, colorful display, and enhanced usability provide a rich environment for monitoring and managing processes effectively. With practical commands allowing for real-time adjustments and intuitive visuals that streamline the information flow, 'htop' empowers system administrators to maintain optimal system performance and swiftly respond to emerging issues. Whether you are new to Linux or a seasoned administrator, incorporating 'htop' into your toolkit will undoubtedly provide a more engaging experience in managing your Linux process landscape, aligning with the goal of nurturing a well-tended process tree akin to caring for an exquisitely shaped bonsai.

5.2. ps and Other Command Line Tools

The command 'ps', short for "process status," is one of the fundamental tools in Linux used for monitoring system processes. This command provides essential information regarding currently running processes, such as the Process ID (PID), user, CPU and memory usage, status, and command name. Unlike 'Top,' which offers a real-time, dynamic view of processes, 'ps' provides a snapshot of processes at a given moment. Understanding the nuances of 'ps' is crucial for effective process management, enabling administrators to swiftly analyze and take action as needed.

One of the reasons 'ps' is so widely used is its flexibility and the variety of options available that tailor its output to specific needs. For instance, the most commonly used invocation is:

```
ps aux
```

This command outputs a comprehensive list of all running processes for all users along with detailed information such as the user owning the process (USER), the CPU and memory usage (%CPU and %MEM), the total time the process has used the CPU (TIME), and the command that initiated the process (COMMAND). Each column can be analyzed to assess current resource consumption, pinpoint potential bottlenecks, and identify processes that may require adjustment or termination.

A pivotal component of 'ps' is the filtering capability it offers through options that allow users to limit the output to particular conditions. For example, using `ps -u username` will filter the processes to show only those owned by the specified user. Additionally, the `-p` option can be utilized to view information about a specific process if you know its PID.

The versatility of 'ps' goes beyond simple checks; it also offers format controls using the `--format` option. This option allows users to customize which columns to display and in what order, enabling tailored views that focus on pertinent data. For example, to see just the PID and command name, you could run:

```
ps -eo pid,comm
```

This level of customization becomes incredibly powerful when used in combination with other command-line tools. For instance, users can pipe the output of 'ps' into more complex processing tools like 'grep' to find specific processes or 'sort' to organize output based on different criteria (like memory usage). For example:

```
ps aux | sort -nrk 4 | head -n 10
```

This command pipeline sorts all processes based on memory usage (%MEM) in descending order and displays the top ten memory-heavy processes.

Moreover, 'ps' can also integrate into scripts for automating monitoring tasks. For instance, administrators can write scripts that trigger alerts should certain processes exceed specified CPU or memory limits. Combining 'ps' with alerting mechanisms, like sending email notifications or logging alerts into a central system, can aid in early detection of performance issues before they become critical.

While 'ps' excels at reporting on currently running processes, it is beneficial to combine it with other command-line tools for a holistic approach to process management. The 'kill' command works in conjunction with 'ps,' allowing administrators to terminate problematic processes identified from 'ps' outputs. For instance, one can find a process ID using 'ps' and pass it then to 'kill':

```
kill <PID>
```

For more aggressive terminations, the 'kill –9 ' command can be used; however, it should be applied judiciously because it does not allow the process to clean up resources.

Additionally, 'ps' sits in a broader context of process management tools within Linux. Commands like 'pstree' provide a hierarchical view of processes, showing parent-child relationships that can be crucial when diagnosing issues related to resource management. Similarly, 'pgrep' can be utilized to find processes based on name pattern matching, while 'pkill' allows for killing processes based on names rather than PID.

In summary, mastering the 'ps' command and associated process management tools is vital for any system administrator or user looking to maintain an efficient Linux environment. With capabilities for real-time analysis, easy integration with other Linux commands, and the potential for automation, 'ps' serves as a foundation for understanding and managing the complex landscape of Linux processes effectively. As you cultivate your administration skills, utilizing 'ps' as part of a comprehensive toolkit empowers you to maintain a balanced system, identifying and addressing potential issues with the same precision and care one would expect when nurturing a bonsai tree.

5.3. Graphical Tools for Process Management

Graphical tools for process management provide a visually intuitive alternative to command-line interfaces like 'top' and 'ps', enhancing the accessibility and ease of use for system administrators and users alike. These tools leverage graphical user interfaces (GUIs) to present process information, system performance metrics, and resource usage in a much more engaging and comprehensible format. In this exploration, we survey some popular graphical tools available for managing processes in Linux environments, highlighting their features, benefits, and use cases.

One of the most widely recognized graphical process management tools is System Monitor. This tool, often included in Linux distributions with desktop environments such as GNOME and KDE, provides an overview of all running processes, resource usage, and system performance metrics. System Monitor typically displays a list of running processes similar to the 'top' command but in a tabular format, showing columns for process ID (PID), user, CPU consumption, memory usage, and command line. Users can easily sort or filter the list based on various criteria, making it simple to identify resource-heavy processes.

In addition to process management, System Monitor often includes graphical representations of CPU and memory usage, displaying real-time information through charts or graphs that allow users to track system performance trends at a glance. This visualization is extremely beneficial for system monitoring over time, enabling administrators to detect issues such as memory leaks or spikes in CPU usage, which might indicate running processes that are excessively consuming resources.

Another option is KSysGuard, a tool specific to the KDE desktop environment that offers enhanced process management capabilities. KSysGuard provides a flexible graphical interface for monitoring system performance, including CPU, memory, network, and disk usage. One standout feature of KSysGuard is the ability to create customizable graphs and monitoring dashboards that can illustrate specific metrics relevant to a user's needs. Users can view and analyze resource consumption not only at a process level but also at the system and user levels.

Additionally, KSysGuard allows users to drill down into individual process details. By double-clicking on a process in its list, users can access detailed statistics, including the process's resource allocation and how it relates to overall system performance. Administrators can also terminate or control processes directly from the KSysGuard interface, enabling swift interventions similar to those available in command-line tools.

For those using the Cinnamon desktop environment, the Cinnamon System Monitor serves as a reliable graphical tool, offering similar functionality as GNOME System Monitor but finely tuned for the Cinnamon aesthetic and workflow. With easy navigation and key features such as real-time process stats, usage summaries, and custom chart displays, Cinnamon System Monitor makes a practical choice for users familiar with the Cinnamon desktop.

Moving beyond traditional monitoring solutions, Glances integrates a more dynamic approach to process management. While Glances is technically a CLI tool, it is also capable of running in a web-based graphical mode, making it accessible from any web browser. Glances provides an overview of system processes and resources in a visually appealing format, allowing users to monitor their system remotely.

One of the striking features of Glances is its ability to adaptively display different metrics based on available screen space. For instance, it can show various performance indicators, such as CPU, memory, disk I/O, and network statistics, all brought together in a single glance —a breath of fresh air when compared to conventional CLI utilities.

When considering virtualization environments, Cockpit emerges as a powerful web-based graphical interface for managing Linux servers, including the ability to track processes. With features designed for ease of use, Cockpit allows administrators to manage systems without extensive command-line knowledge. The dashboard includes performance monitoring capabilities, allowing users to view active processes, system load, CPU utilization, and memory usage in an organized and visually interpretable layout.

Lastly, Psensor provides an excellent option for monitoring temperature and fan speeds alongside process metrics. Psensor can graphically display temperatures from various hardware sensors, including CPU, GPU, and motherboard temperatures, while simultaneously monitoring running processes and their resource usage. The combination of system health metrics with process monitoring provides users with a holistic view of their environment.

In conclusion, the availability of graphical tools for process management in Linux enriches the user experience, enabling quick and effective interaction with system resources. Tools like System Monitor, KSysGuard, and Cockpit provide intuitive graphical interfaces that empower both novice and experienced administrators to monitor and control processes efficiently. As the complexity and demands of Linux systems continue to evolve, these graphical interfaces are increasingly indispensable in ensuring that administrators can maintain optimal system performance with ease. This blend of accessibility and functionality fosters an environment where processes can be managed deliberately and effectively, aligning with the overarching goal of nurturing a well-tended Linux operating system much like an artfully cultivated bonsai tree.

5.4. Integrating Monitoring Tools

Integrating monitoring tools into your Linux system enhances the effectiveness and depth of process management significantly, providing a multi-faceted approach to system diagnostics and performance optimization. As systems grow in complexity and scale, the use of various tools allows administrators to gain broader insights, making proactive decisions towards maintaining efficient and stable environments.

At the core of effective process management is the ability to monitor system performance in real-time. While tools like 'Top' and 'htop' provide essential snapshots of process behavior and resource consumption, integrating additional monitoring solutions allows for a more comprehensive view of system health. For instance, combining process management tools with logging utilities such as syslog or centralized logging solutions provides a historical context to current performance, enabling administrators to identify trends, problems, and anomalies over time.

One approach to enhancing the monitoring system is by utilizing a combination of visualization and alerting tools. For example, employing systems like Grafana and Prometheus allows administrators to collect, store, and visualize metrics from numerous sources in real time. These tools can be configured to track the health of processes along with overall system performance metrics, allowing for interactive dashboards that present essential data at a glance. When thresholds are exceeded, alerts can be triggered, notifying administrators to potential issues before they escalate into critical failures.

Another significant integration involves leveraging container orchestration platforms such as Kubernetes. These platforms often come with robust monitoring capabilities that offer insights into the resource usage of containerized applications. By incorporating tools like the Kubernetes Dashboard alongside traditional process monitors, administrators can effectively track how processes behave within containers, ensuring resource allocation is optimal and aligned with performance expectations. The integration of container monitoring tools like Prometheus with Grafana for visualization can extend this kind of monitoring to individual containers and their resource consumption patterns.

Additionally, configuration management tools such as Ansible or Puppet can tie together monitoring efforts by automating deployments and adjustments based on performance metrics. For instance, if a specific process continually reaches resource limits, Ansible could trigger automated scripts to adjust those limits or alter configurations to mitigate the issue, ensuring that the system remains stable and responsive.

Furthermore, integrating external systems monitoring tools can enhance process oversight. Tools like Nagios or Zabbix facilitate extensive monitoring of processes, networks, and systems, allowing for comprehensive health checks and performance metrics. These tools provide capabilities for checking the status of services, sending notifications if any services become unavailable or if processes consume too many resources.

Moreover, ensuring that monitoring tools integrate smoothly with the existing workflow is essential for optimizing usability. Building an infrastructure that uses Application Programming Interfaces (APIs) can facilitate cross-tool communications. For example, configuring webhooks in monitoring tools to send real-time alerts into team collaboration platforms like Slack provides immediate visibility into process issues without administrators needing to actively check monitoring dashboards.

Finally, as organizations look toward cloud environments, integrating monitoring tools such as AWS CloudWatch, Google Cloud Operations Suite, or Azure Monitor becomes crucial. These tools can track process performance at scale, applying machine learning algorithms to detect outliers dynamically and providing recommendations to improve performance based on historical trends and usage patterns.

As we conclude this exploration of integrating monitoring tools into Linux process management, it's evident that a multi-layered monitoring approach allows for richer insights and proactive management of processes within the system. By combining traditional tools with advanced monitoring frameworks and integrations, administrators can cultivate a finely-tuned environment, much like a bonsai artist sculpting their masterpiece—fostering processes that flourish together with the overall efficacy of the Linux system. Consequently, embracing the integration of diverse monitoring tools supports the ultimate goal of maintaining system robustness, responsiveness, and stability in an increasingly complex operational landscape.

5.5. Interfacing with Third-Party Tools

In a world where process management is an intrinsic element of system stability and efficiency, interfacing with third-party tools becomes increasingly vital for Linux system administrators. These external tools provide enhanced capabilities for monitoring, managing, and optimizing processes beyond what traditional command-line utilities offer. As the demands on Linux environments grow—due to expanded workloads, increasing data volumes, and the need for high availability—finding effective integrations with third-party software can significantly augment the resilience and flexibility of Linux processes.

One core area where third-party tools shine is in comprehensive monitoring. While 'Top' and 'htop' provide essential insights into process activity, solutions such as Nagios, Zabbix, and Prometheus expand monitoring capabilities to cover system-wide health checks, performance metrics, and alerting mechanisms. By integrating these tools, administrators can set thresholds for various metrics—such as CPU load, memory usage, and I/O performance—and receive alerts before these metrics escalate into performance problems. These tools often offer rich graphical interfaces and dashboards that compile data from various sources, allowing for easier analysis and decision-making.

Another key benefit of interfacing with third-party tools is automation and orchestration. Tools like Ansible, Puppet, or Chef enable administrators to automate repetitive tasks associated with process management, such as deploying configurations, managing processes, and ensuring compliance. For example, automating the process of scaling applications based on load using Ansible can not only free up administrative time but can also ensure that systems respond promptly to changes in demand without manual intervention. This level of automation is essential in modern environments leveraging microservices, where processes must adapt to varying workloads dynamically.

In addition to monitoring and automation, specialized performance tuning and optimization tools can significantly enhance process management. Tools such as Sysinternals Suite (and its equivalent for Linux), strace, and perf offer deep insights into process behavior, resource usage, and system calls. By integrating these tools into their workflow, system administrators can diagnose performance bottlenecks by examining how processes utilize system resources and interacting with I/O subsystems. This allows for informed decisions on how to optimize configurations to ensure that processes run efficiently, leading to improved system performance.

Moreover, cloud monitoring and management platforms such as AWS CloudWatch, Azure Monitor, and Google Stackdriver provide critical capabilities for processes running in cloud environments. With many organizations transitioning to hybrid and multi-cloud architectures, being able to interface with these tools becomes essential. They offer features such as automatic scaling based on CPU and memory thresholds, comprehensive logging of process activity, and integrated alerts for unusual behaviors. Leveraging these capabilities ensures that cloud-based processes can be effectively monitored and managed alongside on-premises workloads, promoting seamless operations across environments.

Additionally, integrating security-focused third-party tools like SELinux, AppArmor, or OSSEC provides an added layer of protection by monitoring processes for unauthorized activity. Through these tools, administrators can enforce security policies that dictate which processes can access specific resources and detect any anomalous behaviors. This is increasingly crucial in a landscape where cyber-security threats can target process vulnerabilities, underscoring the importance of robust security in process management.

Dozens of reporting and logging tools such as Splunk, Grafana, or ELK Stack (Elasticsearch, Logstash, Kibana) enhance the observability of process activities. By forwarding logs from processes to these platforms, system administrators can generate insightful reports, visualize trends, and correlate information across different layers of interaction in the system. This comprehensive understanding assists in quickly identifying patterns or issues, leading to faster problem resolution and process optimization efforts.

Lastly, community-driven tools and scripts often play a significant role in process management within Linux environments. Tools like Glances or customized scripts through Bash or Python enable administrators to tailor monitoring and management solutions that fit their specific needs. By tapping into the wealth of shared community knowledge, administrators can enhance their process management capabilities without the overhead of implementing commercial solutions, all while maintaining adaptability for evolving circumstances.

In summary, interfacing with third-party tools greatly enriches Linux process management, providing enhanced monitoring, automation, performance optimization, and security capabilities. Embracing these tools not only allows for proactive management of processes but also fosters community involvement and knowledge sharing. As system administrators hone their skills in integrating these tools into their processes, they create a dynamic environment that can respond to system demands with agility and precision. This strategic integration guarantees a resilient and effective Linux environment, much like a well-tended bonsai that thrives through thoughtful care and adaptation to its surroundings. Through this journey into the world of third-party tools, administrators will find themselves better equipped to navigate the complexity of Linux processes while ensuring optimal performance and stability for their systems.

6. Pruning Processes: Ethics and Best Practices

6.1. Understanding Process Load

Understanding process load in Linux systems is an essential aspect of effective system administration. It entails recognizing what constitutes process bloat, managing resource distribution, and making informed decisions about which processes to prioritize or terminate based on their load and impact on overall system functionality. As we navigate this intricate landscape, we'll break down the components that shape our understanding of process load and highlight strategies to manage it effectively.

At its core, process load refers to the demands that different processes place on system resources, including CPU time, memory usage, disk I/O, and network bandwidth. As these processes compete for limited resources, the total load they generate can significantly influence the performance and responsiveness of a Linux system. High process load typically leads to sluggishness, increased latency, or even complete system unresponsiveness, which is why recognizing and addressing it is crucial for maintaining system health.

One clear indicator of process load is the CPU usage metrics. In this context, we must evaluate whether individual processes are utilizing an excessive share of CPU cycles. A single process consuming a disproportionate amount of CPU can lead to process bloat; for example, a runaway process might consume nearly 100% of the available CPU time, thereby starving other processes of the resources they require. Monitoring tools such as 'top' and 'htop' can provide insights into CPU percentages consumed by each process, allowing administrators to identify potential culprits that may need attention.

In addition to CPU usage, memory consumption is a critical aspect to consider when assessing process load. Processes that utilize a high amount of RAM can exhaust available memory resources, leading to swapping and degraded system performance. When memory usage climbs to critical levels, the kernel may invoke the Out-Of-Memory

(OOM) killer to terminate processes, which can significantly disrupt system operations. Therefore, regular monitoring of memory usage, specifically identifying processes with growing memory footprints, is essential for preventing process bloat from overwhelming available resources.

Disk I/O is another essential factor in evaluating process load. Processes that engage heavily in read/write operations can become bottlenecks, significantly impacting system performance. Thorough monitoring of disk usage patterns can illuminate processes that perform unnecessary or redundant operations, thus enabling administrators to take corrective action, whether that means optimizing file access patterns or adjusting configurations.

Network bandwidth can also contribute to process load, particularly in server environments where processes must handle incoming and outgoing traffic. Processes that engage in excessive network communication lead to congestion, which can hinder overall performance levels. Monitoring network utilization can reveal whether specific applications or services inadvertently consume too much bandwidth, just as they might do with CPU or memory.

Understanding process load isn't just about metrics; it also involves evaluating the relationships between processes and their states. Processes can be found in various states: running, waiting, or sleeping, among others. Analyzing how many processes are in waiting states can provide insights into resource contention issues. If many processes are waiting on I/O operations, for instance, it may indicate a throughput problem on the disk, prompting a closer inspection of disk activity and load balancing.

Another critical aspect of managing process load is interpreting system-wide load averages, usually presented as three figures that represent the average system load over the last 1, 5, and 15 minutes. Understanding these averages in conjunction with the number of available CPU cores is crucial. If the load average is persistently higher than the number of CPU cores, it generally signifies that the system is overloaded. In contrast, a sustained load average lower than available cores suggests the system is likely operating within healthy parameters.

In evaluating what constitutes process bloat, administrators need to establish thresholds tailored to their specific environments. A process consuming 20% CPU usage could be acceptable in certain contexts, whereas the same consumption might be problematic in environments with limited resources. Setting these parameters involves taking into account the expected workloads, critical application requirements, and how the specific processes interact with overall system resources.

Finally, creating a well-structured approach for managing process load necessitates the integration of tools that support monitoring and punitive actions. Automation scripts could be employed to track resource usage trends, alerting administrators when specific thresholds are breached, allowing for proactive engagement before system health deteriorates. Combining these insights with a deeper understanding of process management principles empowers administrators to make informed decisions, ensuring that performance remains optimal and processes remain within acceptable limits.

In summary, understanding process load is a dynamic and continuous endeavor that goes beyond surface metrics. It requires thorough monitoring, analytical practices, and proactive engagement to maintain a healthy and responsive Linux system. By dissecting process contributions to resource usage and defining clear parameters for acceptable performance, administrators can prevent process bloat and cultivate a seamless operational environment, much like the undisrupted aesthetic of a carefully pruned bonsai. This nuanced approach will ultimately prove invaluable in navigating the complex landscape of process management and system administration.

6.2. Deciding When to Kill a Process

As a system administrator navigating the complexities of process management, determining when to kill a process is a fundamental skill that lies at the heart of maintaining an efficient and stable Linux environment. This decision-making process requires a careful assessment of various factors, including resource allocation, process behavior, and overall system health. Understanding how to set parameters for process termination can help create a structured approach, guiding administrators as they balance operational priorities and performance demands.

The essence of deciding to kill a process falls into three critical categories: evaluation of system performance, assessment of process impact, and consideration of organizational protocols. Each of these areas provides a framework for making informed decisions regarding which processes to terminate, enhancing overall system efficiency.

Evaluating system performance involves monitoring key metrics that signal when a process may be causing issues. Utilization of tools like 'Top,' 'htop,' and 'ps' allows administrators to access real-time information about CPU usage, memory consumption, and input/output operations. High CPU utilization by a specific process may indicate it is consuming excessive resources at the expense of other critical tasks. Additionally, monitoring memory usage can unveil processes that lead to high memory consumption or swapping, allowing for timely intervention before performance degrades. Conversely, processes that are consistently idle or in a suspended state may be good candidates for termination, especially if they do not contribute to essential operations.

Next, assessing the impact of a process on overall system functionality is crucial for identifying the right candidates for termination. Some processes, despite high resource usage, may be mission-critical, such as web server processes handling user requests. Terminating such processes can adversely affect users and lead to service disruptions, which is something to consider seriously before taking action. In contrast, processes that are identified as rogue or misbehaving can significantly affect stability and performance, making them appropriate targets for termination. Additionally, processes spawned from applications that have crashed or are no longer responding should also be evaluated for termination to free up system resources.

It's equally important to take organizational protocols into account before deciding to kill a process. Many organizations will have established best practices regarding process management, including guidelines on acceptable resource usage or standard operating procedures for troubleshooting high-load situations. These policies may dictate how much resource consumption is permissible or when a process should be automatically flagged for administrative attention. Having a documented procedure can mitigate risks when terminating processes, ensuring consistency in approach and communication with other team members.

In addition to evaluating performance, assessing root causes is vital in the decision-making process. A process may exhibit high resource usage due to factors such as poor programming practices, inefficient algorithms, or simply an overload of requests. Understanding and addressing these root causes, rather than simply terminating a process, can improve overall system health and prevent a repeat of the issue in the future. In some cases, it may be prudent to alter the configuration of a process—adjusting its scheduling, priority, or resource allocation —rather than forcibly killing it.

When making the decision to kill a process, it's important to consider the implications of using different signals. The default signal for killing a process (SIGTERM) requests a graceful shutdown, providing the process an opportunity to clean up its resources. Conversely, sending a SIGKILL signal forces immediate termination, which can lead to resource leaks or data corruption, depending on the nature of the process. Administrators should weigh these options carefully, understanding the consequences of each approach.

Moreover, it's vital to foster an environment where communication is prioritized within teams when processes are approaching termination. Providing clarity about why a process is being killed and the rationale behind the decision can help foster trust among team members. Furthermore, after a process is terminated, it's good practice to document the circumstances that led to the decision and any follow-up actions that were taken. This record-keeping not only provides context for future reference but also contributes to a culture of continuous improvement within the organization.

Ultimately, the decision to kill a process should be rooted in a clear understanding of situational context derived from monitoring tools, organizational policies, and best practices. By setting parameters for process termination, administrators can navigate the complex landscape of resource management with confidence, ensuring that the balance between performance, user satisfaction, and system stability remains intact. Adopting a structured approach equips administrators with the framework necessary to maintain operational resilience and adaptability—qualities that are paramount in the ever-evolving world of Linux process management.

6.3. Ethical Considerations in Process Management

In the domain of process management, ethical considerations are of paramount importance as they guide system administrators in their roles as stewards of resources and maintainers of operational integrity. As administrators navigate the complex landscape of process monitoring, management, and resource allocation, they carry the responsibility of ensuring that their actions do not compromise system stability, user privacy, or overall performance. This section explores the ethical implications of process management, emphasizing a holistic approach that balances organizational needs with individual rights and ethical standards.

At the heart of ethical process management lies the responsibility to manage shared resources fairly. In a multi-user environment, processes can belong to different users, each representing a distinct set of needs and priorities. As processes contend for CPU time, memory, I/O operations, and network bandwidth, system administrators must strive to allocate resources equitably. Favoring one user or process over another can lead to performance degradation, user frustration, and can even disrupt business operations. Ethical stewardship involves implementing fair policies and practices that not only optimize system performance but also respect the rights and needs of all users.

Moreover, transparency is a crucial ethical consideration in process management. Administrators should maintain clear communication regarding system status, resource allocation policies, and any actions taken to terminate or adjust processes. Users should be informed when their processes are consuming excessive resources, and they should understand the rationale for any administrative decisions. This transparency cultivates trust between users and administrators, fostering a collaborative environment where individuals feel involved in maintaining system health.

Security and privacy also play a significant role in ethical process management. Administrators must ensure that processes do not jeopardize sensitive information or expose the system to vulnerabilities. The ability to monitor user processes should be exercised judiciously, respecting user privacy while balancing the need to ensure system integrity. Implementing robust security policies and access controls not only protects data but also reinforces an ethical approach to process management that prioritizes user rights.

The implications of terminating processes add another layer of ethical complexity. Killing a process may be necessary to restore system performance or rectify a misbehaving application, but it should be done with care. Expedited decisions to terminate processes without consideration may lead to data loss or disruption of critical operations. An ethical framework dictates that administrators take a measured approach—assessing the impact of termination, exploring alternative solutions, and ensuring that, whenever possible, processes are gracefully shut down to prevent adverse consequences.

Additionally, administrators are tasked with managing the impact of high-load processes on system performance. While it may be tempting to arbitrarily kill resource-intensive applications, administrators should seek to address the root causes of high resource consumption.

This may mean working with developers to optimize application performance or adjusting configurations to minimize the impact of specific processes. Such practices not only enhance system efficiency but also demonstrate an ethical commitment to fostering improvement rather than resorting to punitive actions.

Ethics in process management extends to the development and implement of best practices and guidelines for managing processes. By establishing standard operating procedures, performance baselines, and a clear set of criteria for acceptable resource usage, administrators can create a structured framework that guides decision-making. This aids in aligning process management actions with ethical principles, ensuring that all users experience consistent and fair treatment across the system.

Lastly, continuous learning and education around ethical considerations in process management are vital. Administrators should stay informed of emerging trends, best practices, and ethical dilemmas in the realm of technology and system administration. Professional development opportunities and training centered on ethics can help administrators navigate potential conflicts and enhance their understanding of the broader implications of their actions.

In summary, ethical considerations in process management require a comprehensive approach that balances efficiency, user needs, and system integrity. By committing to fairness in resource allocation, maintaining transparency, upholding security and privacy standards, and taking measured actions in process management, system administrators can foster an ethical and collaborative environment. This dedication to ethical stewardship ultimately enhances the overall health of the system and strengthens the relationship between administrators and users, creating a resilient and productive operational space where everyone can thrive.

6.4. Best Practices for Process Pruning

Establishing best practices for process pruning is an essential skill for any Linux system administrator aiming to maintain a healthy, efficient computing environment. These practices ensure that the active process landscape remains manageable, optimized, and responsive to the needs of users and applications. Below, we will explore various best practices for process pruning, focusing on systematic approaches, routine enhancements, and strategic interventions that keep the system performing at its best.

Firstly, it is vital to have a comprehensive understanding of the processes running on your system before embarking on any pruning activities. This involves using tools like 'top', 'htop', 'ps', and others to get a complete overview of all running processes, their respective resource usage, and their states. Regularly monitoring this information is a necessary prerequisite for effective pruning, allowing administrators to identify processes that are consuming excessive resources or behaving unexpectedly. Establishing baseline metrics for acceptable process resource utilization can also facilitate more informed decisions when invoking pruning actions.

Once a clear picture of system processes is established, it is beneficial to create guidelines specifying criteria for pruning decisions. This might include setting thresholds for CPU usage, memory consumption, or process responsiveness. For instance, a process that consistently uses over a certain percentage of CPU resources for an extended period might be flagged for review or termination. These guidelines help streamline the process of identifying which processes need attention and reduce the potential for arbitrary or hasty pruning actions.

Implementing a routine for process analysis and review is also paramount. This routine could be scheduled at regular intervals to systematically assess process behavior over time. Automated scripts can help in logging resource usage patterns to provide visibility into trends. For example, a cron job could analyze resource utilization daily and generate a report highlighting processes that consistently exceed pre-defined thresholds. Regularly re-evaluating these patterns ensures that previously benign processes are re-examined as the system evolves or as workloads change.

Documentation plays a critical role in effective process management. Keeping detailed records of processes that have been pruned, including their resource usage and the rationale behind their termination, creates a valuable repository of knowledge. This helps in understanding the impact of specific processes on system performance and allows for refining pruning policies over time. Moreover, this documentation can facilitate communication within teams, providing insights into resource management decisions for team members or future administrators.

Beyond routine pruning, utilizing user feedback is essential in managing processes effectively. Users often have insights into which processes may not be functioning correctly or are consuming unnecessary resources. Implementing a systematic feedback mechanism, such as a simple reporting tool integrated into the user interface, can allow non-technical users to inform administrators about processes they perceive as problematic. Participating in a dialogue with users fosters a collaborative approach to resource management, ensuring that pruning decisions align with the operational needs of the organization.

Important as it is, pruning should be approached with care—making decisions on process termination requires understanding potential ramifications. Some processes may play crucial roles that are not immediately apparent. For example, a process with high CPU utilization may be a legitimate part of a critical application, possibly indicating the need for additional resources rather than termination. Before deciding to kill a process, consider investigating the underlying issues through diagnostic tools or seeking consultation from affected users to inform your decision-making process.

Security implications are another key consideration in pruning practices. Processes may have different permission levels based on user roles or security profiles. Continuously monitoring processes for unauthorized access or abnormal behavior helps prevent potential security breaches. Implementing security measures, such as employing SELinux or AppArmor filters on critical processes ensures that pruning actions do not compromise system security, creating a balance between performance and protection.

Furthermore, after executing pruning actions, it's vital to actively monitor the system's behavior and responsiveness post-intervention. Immediately following a termination event, administrators should check overall system performance and user satisfaction to ensure the correct processes have been managed. Tools like user satisfaction surveys or performance metrics can shed light on whether the pruning has had the desired outcome or if additional changes are necessary.

Lastly, proactively preparing for process overload situations via preventive measures is instrumental. Consider employing load balancers or setting up auto-scaling solutions for critical applications to manage resource demands dynamically. Employing a strategy that includes built-in alerts when predetermined thresholds are met can skirt issues that necessitate process pruning altogether, allowing systems to respond to resource constraints before they escalate to the point of requiring drastic measures.

In conclusion, best practices for process pruning in Linux environments revolve around systematic observation, routine assessments, and informed decision-making. By establishing guidelines, fostering user engagement, documenting actions, and maintaining a proactive approach, administrators can optimize the process landscape for enhanced system performance and stability. With diligent pruning practices in place, the process tree can be maintained meticulously, allowing Linux environments to run smoothly, support user needs, and respond effectively to changing workloads. Ensuring the health of the system through regular maintenance ultimately leads to a more resilient and robust operational capacity, mirroring the careful nurturing that defines the art of bonsai cultivation.

6.5. Case Studies in Effective Pruning

In the domain of effective process management, case studies provide invaluable insights into the practical application of strategies discussed throughout this book. By examining real-world examples of both successes and failures, we gain a richer understanding of how to navigate the complexities of the Linux process tree and the essential art of pruning processes. These cases serve not only as illustrative narratives but also as learning opportunities that shape best practices, guiding administrators in their decision-making processes.

The first example highlights a medium-sized web hosting company faced with scalability issues due to inefficient resource utilization. Over time, their server load had increased significantly, leading to slow response times and frequent complaints from customers. The team decided to employ process pruning strategies to improve overall system performance.

They began by utilizing monitoring tools such as 'Top' and 'htop' to identify processes consuming excess CPU and memory. Their analysis revealed that outdated background services, which were no longer in use, were still running and consuming valuable resources. Additionally, they noticed rogue scripts from a poorly coded web application that spiked CPU usage when triggered. The team documented these findings and developed a strategy for safely terminating the unnecessary services and debugging the application.

After executing the termination of the idle processes, the administrators implemented more rigorous monitoring protocols to track the behavior of critical applications. They established routine audits of running processes, allowing them to proactively manage resource allocation. The decision to prune inactive processes not only improved response times but also elevated user satisfaction significantly.

Next, consider a case study from a large financial institution where security concerns are paramount. This organization faced challenges with managing processes that had been compromised by malware, leading to unauthorized access and potential data breaches. The IT team recognized the urgent need to implement stricter process management practices to safeguard sensitive information.

To effectively manage their processes, the institution deployed a combination of security-focused and monitoring tools, including SELinux and Nagios, alongside traditional process monitoring solutions like 'ps' and 'top'. Through comprehensive audits, they identified several malicious processes that were running, hidden under similar names to legitimate applications. The team carried out a strategic pruning, terminating the malicious processes and isolating the affected systems from the network.

Beyond immediate termination, the security team conducted root cause analysis to understand how the breach occurred. They identified vulnerabilities related to outdated software and insufficient user permissions. As a proactive measure, they established new protocols for ongoing monitoring and initiated regular security training for staff, ensuring awareness of common threats. The case study emphasizes the importance of ethical considerations in process management, illustrating how terminating processes was part of a larger strategy to protect users and their data.

The third case study originates from a cloud service provider that catered to customers with variable workloads, necessitating a flexible approach to process management. With the inception of a new client project anticipated to spike resource usage, the administrators faced the challenge of managing dynamic processes across virtual environments efficiently.

Recognizing the limitations of static resource allocation, the administrators researched and implemented dynamic resource allocation tools, including Kubernetes, which automatically scaled processes based on demand. They also integrated Prometheus for robust monitoring of active processes, along with Grafana for real-time visualization of system performance metrics.

During the project's initial phase, the automated system proved invaluable in adapting to sudden traffic surges. By efficiently provisioning cloud resources and managing processes dynamically, the provider could maintain performance levels that met customer expectations without over-provisioning resources. This adaptive approach illustrated the benefits of integrating automation within process management, ultimately leading to greater operational efficiency and client satisfaction.

Finally, a manufacturing company released an update to a critical application that led to unexpected performance issues caused by a single resource-intensive process. Administrators noticed an increase in overall system load from monitoring tools, which negatively impacted other processes within the production environment. A robust troubleshooting effort ensued, centering around understanding process dependencies and interactions.

Employing extensive logging and advanced tools like strace, the team was able to pinpoint the root cause of the performance degradation. Their investigation revealed that the newly updated application inadvertently initiated a sub-process that created a bottleneck. By restructuring the process flow and adjusting the scheduling of dependent processes, the administrators could mitigate the impact of the erroneous code.

This study underlines the significance of diagnosing process relationships and dependencies in effective process management, coupling technical knowledge with an awareness of potential impacts throughout the system.

In conclusion, case studies in effective pruning illustrate the complexity and nuances of Linux process management. They provide real-world contexts for the best practices discussed, showcasing scenarios that emphasize the importance of proactive monitoring, ethical decision-making, and strategy implementation. These insights encourage a growth mindset among system administrators, fostering an environment where continuous learning and adaptation lead to successful process management outcomes. By integrating lessons learned from these case studies, Linux administrators can refine their process management strategies, creating a responsive and efficient operational environment that stands resilient against evolving challenges.

7. Process Accounting and User Management

7.1. Tracking Process Activity

Tracking process activity is a fundamental aspect of effective system administration in Linux environments. By closely monitoring which processes are running and how they utilize system resources, administrators gain critical insights necessary for maintaining optimal system performance. This section outlines various techniques and tools for accounting for process usage effectively, ensuring that the system remains responsive and resource-efficient.

To begin with, it's essential to know which tools to utilize for tracking process activity. One of the most powerful tools available for this task is the 'top' command. This dynamic, real-time utility provides a comprehensive overview of current processes, showcasing the CPU and memory usage of each. By default, 'top' sorts processes based on their CPU consumption, allowing administrators to immediately pinpoint resource hogs. Users can interact with 'top' to change the sorting criteria, look at processes by memory usage, and apply filters as needed to narrow down their focus.

Another useful command is 'htop,' an advanced alternative to 'top.' Htop enhances the user experience with a colorful, user-friendly interface that displays processes in a way that is easier to understand at a glance. It also provides additional functionality, such as a tree view of process hierarchies and the ability to interactively adjust process priorities through its interface. With htop, administrators can more readily visualize and manage the relationships between parent and child processes.

In addition to command-line utilities, administrators may turn to graphical tools such as System Monitor, KSysGuard, or Cockpit for process tracking. These tools often come packaged with Linux distributions and provide intuitive visualizations of running processes, resource usage, and system performance metrics. The graphical representation of data simplifies process monitoring and can be particularly useful for those who may not be comfortable using command-line interfaces.

An integral part of tracking process activity also involves logging and accounting features that record process behavior over time. Utilizing the 'ps' command allows administrators to snapshot process states at specific points, which can be useful for benchmarking or for historical reference when diagnosing issues. The command can be customized with options like 'aux' to provide detailed information about all processes, regardless of ownership. By scripting regular 'ps' commands, administrators can automate the logging of system states, allowing for more sophisticated analysis of process activity patterns over time.

In addition to these basic tools, employing more advanced monitoring solutions can enhance tracking capabilities significantly. Tools like Prometheus combined with Grafana allow for extensive monitoring of metrics over time, enabling administrators to not only visualize real-time data but also establish historical trends. These solutions can gather metrics from various sources, making it easier to see system-wide impacts of individual processes.

Integrating process accounting systems is another strategy for tracking usage. Tools like 'acct' can be utilized to monitor and collect data on process execution. When implemented, these tools log the resources consumed by each process in detail, which can later be analyzed to determine which processes are driving resource usage and how efficiently the system is operating.

Another critical consideration when monitoring processes is setting appropriate alert thresholds. Administrators should determine key metrics that, when exceeded, should trigger alerts. For example, if a process's CPU usage exceeds a certain percentage over a sustained period, it may indicate an issue that needs immediate attention. Establishing automated alerts using tools like Nagios or Zabbix can help ensure that administrators are promptly informed of potential system performance problems.

Lastly, it is essential to foster a proactive monitoring culture. Administrators should regularly review process logs and usage patterns to identify trends that could inform future capacity planning. This ongoing vigilance can help avoid scenarios where a process unexpectedly overwhelms system resources or where performance problems are allowed to escalate before corrective action is taken.

In conclusion, tracking process activity is a multifaceted task that requires the effective use of a variety of tools and strategies. By employing a combination of command-line utilities, graphical interfaces, comprehensive monitoring solutions, and proactive alerting mechanisms, Linux administrators can maintain a finely-tuned system. Doing so not only ensures optimal performance but also fosters an environment that supports successful process management—similar to the meticulous care one would exercise in nurturing a flourishing bonsai tree. By continuously honing their skills and monitoring capabilities, administrators can adeptly manage processes that sustain the operational health of Linux environments.

7.2. User Permissions and Process Control

User Permissions and Process Control

In the intricate dance of process management within Linux systems, user roles play a pivotal part in determining whose processes control system resources and how these resources are managed. Understanding user permissions and the associated impact on process control is essential for maintaining system integrity, security, and efficiency. This section explores how user roles affect process management, the nuances of permissions, and best practices for ensuring a balanced and secure environment.

At the heart of process control is the concept of user privileges, which dictates the actions a user can perform on a system. Linux is built on a foundation of multi-user capabilities, meaning that multiple individuals can interact with the system concurrently, each running their own processes. User permissions are set through three primary levels: owner, group, and others, with each level having distinct rights to read, write, and execute files or processes.

When a user initiates a process, it runs with the permissions associated with their user account. This context is critical, as it ensures that processes only have access to resources allowed by the user's permissions. For example, a regular user may not possess the rights to start processes that require system-level access such as modifying critical system files or spying on other users' processes. Thus, any misappropriation of user permissions can potentially lead to security vulnerabilities, where a user gains unintended access to resources inappropriate for their role.

The effective management of process control through user permissions starts with the principle of least privilege. This security concept suggests that users should only be granted the minimum necessary permissions to perform their tasks. By strictly adhering to this principle, administrators can limit the risk of accidental or malicious actions that could compromise system integrity. For instance, if a user is only allowed to run applications within a specified directory, they cannot inadvertently alter sensitive system files, reducing overall risk.

Moreover, process ownership plays a critical role in managing system resources and actions taken against these processes. Every running process in Linux has a user ID (UID) linked with it, which corresponds to the user who initiated it. This association ensures that only the owning user can directly manage or terminate their processes, barring actions by privileged users like root. As a result, understanding the user permissions associated with processes becomes vital in contexts where many users share the same system resources.

Another important consideration is the use of setuid programs. In Linux, setuid is a permission that allows ordinary users to execute specific programs with escalated privileges, effectively running with the permissions of the file owner, often root. While setuid is useful for enabling certain functionalities, it presents an inherent risk; if a malicious actor gains control over a setuid program, they can exploit it to execute harmful actions at a higher privilege level. Consequently, administrators must exercise caution when employing setuid binaries and ensure they are secure, well-audited, and necessary for operational needs.

Effective auditing and monitoring of process activity based on user permissions is a critical discipline. By utilizing tools like `auditd` or the Linux Audit framework, administrators can log access to privileged processes and monitor any attempts to run restricted operations. Regularly reviewing these logs not only aids in identifying unauthorized access attempts but also forms part of a comprehensive security posture that protects against privilege escalation attacks.

In environments where multiple users frequently execute processes with overlapping resource needs, resource management becomes increasingly complex. For instance, when designing multi-user systems or services where various users run their own applications, it's crucial to define clear resource limits for each user or group. Using control groups, or cgroups, allows administrators to set limits on CPU and memory usage for specific users or groups. This ensures that no single user monopolizes system resources, fostering a more equitable environment that supports all users and services effectively.

Furthermore, it's essential to create a culture of awareness around permissions and process control among users. Through training and regular communication, users should understand the significance of adhering to assigned permissions and the dangers of circumventing established protocols. Cultivating a sense of responsibility among users reduces the probability of security incidents and enhances cooperation in maintaining a healthy system.

Lastly, system administrators should regularly review user permissions and access levels, adjusting them as necessary based on changing roles and responsibilities or after security incident analyses. Keeping this dynamic helps ensure that permissions reflect current operational needs while safeguarding against stale accounts or previously granted privileges that are no longer applicable.

In conclusion, user permissions and process control are inextricably linked in the Linux environment. User roles dictate which processes can run, what resources they can access, and how they interact with other system operations. By implementing best practices centered on the principle of least privilege, conducting thorough monitoring, and proactively managing permissions, administrators can create a stable and secure process environment. Just as a bonsai artist meticulously shapes their artwork, so too must system administrators diligently oversee user permissions and process controls, ensuring that Linux systems flourish gracefully in their operational priorities.

7.3. Managing Resource Distribution

Managing Resource Distribution on a Linux system requires a careful balancing act, akin to an artist meticulously arranging elements within a composition. Resources—comprising CPU cycles, memory, I/O operations, and network bandwidth—are finite, and improper distribution can lead to performance degradation, application failures, or system-wide slowdowns. Effective resource management is not just about allocating more resources but rather involves strategic oversight, continuous monitoring, and adaptive responses based on user needs and process demands.

The first cornerstone of effective resource distribution is establishing an accurate understanding of resource demands across applications and processes. Implementing a comprehensive monitoring solution that provides real-time insights into resource usage patterns is essential. Tools such as 'top', 'htop', and 'glances' offer dynamic visuals of current usage and allow you to identify which processes consume the most CPU or memory at any given time. Meanwhile, logging solutions combined with monitoring dashboards, like those provided by Grafana and Prometheus, assist administrators in assessing trends over longer periods. Regularly analyzing historical data can reveal usage spikes or patterns that inform better resource allocation decisions.

Another key aspect is setting resource limits and thresholds based on observed usage. In a multi-user environment, it may be prudent to delineate available resources through techniques like cgroups (control groups) in Linux. Cgroups enable administrators to allocate specific amounts of CPU, memory, and I/O to individual users or groups of processes, ensuring that no single process can monopolize system resources. By carefully defining these limits based on workload requirements, you create an environment where resources are shared equitably, minimizing the risk of performance bottlenecks and shared-resource contention.

In dynamically resource-rich environments, such as in cloud computing or virtualization, scaling resources becomes critical. Tools that provide dynamic resource allocation capabilities—like Kubernetes—allow administrators to adjust resource limits and increase CPU or memory allocations when demand peaks. This responsive scaling is crucial for applications with variable loads, ensuring that resource availability aligns with fluctuating user demands. An adaptive resource allocation strategy minimizes waste while maintaining performance levels under varying conditions.

Furthermore, resource distribution must also encompass network bandwidth. Process management often involves ensuring that no single user or process consumes excessive bandwidth at the expense of others. Implementing Quality of Service (QoS) policies can be an effective strategy for prioritizing traffic, helping to maintain performance for critical applications while limiting the impact of less urgent processes. By monitoring network usage alongside CPU and memory consumption, administrators can intervene before bandwidth issues affect user experiences.

Automation is another key element of effective resource distribution. Applications should be designed to automatically request additional resources as needed or release them when they are not in use. Implementing automation tools and scripts enables a more proactive approach; these mechanisms can adjust resources based on predefined criteria or thresholds, thereby alleviating the administrative burden of continually monitoring and adjusting allocations. Such strategic automation ensures that optimal resource distribution is maintained with minimal intervention.

Moreover, ensure that user needs and process priorities are consistently aligned. Frequent communication with users about resource requirements is essential. Users may be unaware of resource-heavy applications or services running in their sessions, leading to unnecessary strain on the system. By establishing a dialogue, administrators can better understand which processes require additional resources and which ones can be pruned or optimized.

Lastly, be mindful of the potential for conflicts when managing resource distribution. In environments where competing processes vie for the same resources, conflicts can arise, leading to inefficiencies or failures. Monitoring tools should be equipped to identify such conflicts early, allowing administrators to make real-time adjustments to correct course. This may entail altering priorities between processes, temporarily suspending less critical tasks, or redirecting resource allocations depending on immediate system health.

In conclusion, managing resource distribution in a Linux environment is a multifaceted challenge that requires strategic planning, constant vigilance, and the integration of effective monitoring and automation tools. By establishing a framework for understanding resource allocations, defining limits, implementing dynamic scaling, and engaging with users, administrators can cultivate a balanced and productive system. Through these practices, the landscape of resource distribution can be managed not just for efficiency but for resilience—ensuring that processes flourish within an environment designed to support their needs, much like a bonsai shape to perfection through careful and considered pruning.

7.4. Balancing User and Process Needs

Balancing user and process needs is a critical consideration for any system administrator tasked with maintaining an optimal Linux environment. This balance ensures that individual user requirements are met while simultaneously preserving overall system performance and stability. As processes vie for system resources, effective management becomes essential to avoid contention and to foster a responsive and efficient operating system.

In a multi-user Linux environment, multiple processes are often competing for the same resources, such as CPU cycles, memory, and I/O operations. Each user may run different applications that have varying resource demands, leading to potential conflicts. Therefore, it is imperative to understand both user-level and process-level priorities to devise a suitable strategy for resource allocation.

The first step toward balancing user and process needs involves thorough monitoring of resource usage at both levels. Utilizing tools like 'top', 'htop', and system logging software enables administrators to collect real-time data about which users are consuming the most resources and how their processes are performing. Understanding patterns in resource usage allows for informed decision-making when it comes to optimizing system performance without compromising user expectations.

Setting clear priorities and limits is another cornerstone of this balancing act. Administrators can implement quotas to restrict the amount of CPU and memory that any single user can consume, thereby preventing resource hogs from affecting the performance of other users' processes. These limits should be carefully tailored based on normal usage patterns—essentially establishing a baseline for acceptable resource use. By doing this, you create a safeguard against any single process overwhelming system resources.

Moreover, user education plays a crucial role in achieving balance. Users should be informed about how their actions may affect overall system performance and should be encouraged to manage the processes they run responsibly. For instance, introducing best practices for running resource-intensive applications during off-peak hours can significantly reduce overall system load and conflicts between users' processes. This proactive approach not only benefits the system but also cultivates a cooperative environment among users.

In addition to limiting resource use and educating users, implementing process scheduling can also help balance user needs. The Linux kernel employs various scheduling algorithms that can be adjusted to assign priorities to processes dynamically. Administrators can leverage the nice and renice commands to adjust the priority of processes based on their urgency and importance. Higher-priority processes would then compete less for CPU time, enhancing responsiveness for critical applications while ensuring that lower-priority tasks have their needs met without causing delays to more important processes.

Furthermore, administrators can utilize load balancing strategies across multiple servers or instances in a distributed environment. By intelligently distributing user processes and jobs across available resources, you can effectively manage peak loads while maintaining performance. This architecture ensures no single server becomes a bottleneck, enhancing the overall efficiency of system operations.

When it comes to process termination, understanding when to take action is also critical in maintaining balance. If a particular process is detected to be hindering overall performance—potentially due to excessive resource consumption—administrators must weigh the consequences of terminating that process against the needs of the user who initiated it. This requires careful evaluation of the impact on users and the overall system. As such, applying appropriate metrics and thresholds will help guide decisions on when and how to intervene.

Establishing a robust incident response mechanism allows for quick action when performance issues arise, enabling administrators to maintain balance in resource allocation dynamically. Implementing logging and alerting systems can notify administrators of unusual process behavior or excessive resource consumption, allowing them to intervene before problems escalate.

Lastly, continuous assessment of user and process needs, as well as regular updates to protocols and quotas, is crucial as workloads change over time. As new applications are introduced and user behaviors evolve, administrators must remain vigilant to adapt to changing circumstances to ensure the balance persists.

In conclusion, balancing user and process needs in Linux environments requires an understanding of resource allocation, user behaviors, and effective monitoring practices. By employing strategic limits, proactive education, and dynamic scheduling, administrators can create a responsive system that meets user demands while maintaining overall integrity and performance. This finely-tuned equilibrium not only enhances system usability but also fosters a collaborative atmosphere where both administrators and users can work harmoniously— akin to the delicate balance required in nurturing a flourishing bonsai tree. This ongoing commitment to balance will ensure that the Linux process landscape remains both healthy and efficient in the face of evolving challenges.

7.5. Security Implications of Process Management

In the dynamic and complex landscape of Linux system administration, the security implications of process management cannot be overlooked. Every process running on a system has potential security risks associated with it, whether from internal sources, such as poorly coded applications, or external threats exploiting system vulnerabilities. Understanding these risks is vital for any administrator looking to create a stable and secure environment.

One of the primary security risks within process management is unauthorized access to sensitive processes. Processes can be manipulated or monitored, and if a malicious actor gains unauthorized access to a running process, they can potentially hijack the process and access its resources, including sensitive data. This emphasizes the importance of strict user permission management. Processes should run under the least privilege principle—ensuring that no process has more access than necessary to perform its functions.

As administrators configure process ownership, they should be diligent in ensuring that processes are executed by users or system accounts endowed with the minimum required permissions. For instance, processes requiring elevated privileges should be designed to run under a dedicated service account with limited access. It's also advisable to regularly audit user permissions and process ownership to mitigate the risk of privilege escalation attacks.

Another significant concern lies in shared resources, particularly in multi-user or multi-application environments. Processes that operate in shared environments must be carefully managed to prevent one process from negatively impacting others, as excessive consumption of resources can lead to Denial of Service (DoS) conditions. This necessitates process isolation techniques, such as containers or virtualization, that cleanly separate processes and limit their access to shared system resources. Technologies like Docker or Kubernetes enable administrators to create isolated environments for application processes, thus protecting the overall system integrity.

Moreover, the typical behavior of processes can sometimes be indicative of malicious activity. Anomalies such as unexpected resource consumption patterns, process executions at irregular times, or processes attempting to access sensitive files can all signal a potential security threat. Consequently, administrators should implement monitoring solutions that track process behavior and alert them to suspicious activities. Tools like auditd can monitor process interactions, giving administrators insights into potential misuse or compromise.

In environments where services must be accessible over a network, it is critical to secure application processes against external threats. This necessitates the use of secure coding practices to reduce vulnerabilities in applications that can be exploited remotely. Processes running web servers or applications frequently become main targets for attackers hoping to exploit common vulnerabilities found in services exposed to the internet. Routine security assessments, including penetration tests and vulnerability scans, can help identify and remediate weaknesses.

Implementing robust logging and auditing mechanisms also bolsters security in process management. By maintaining logs of process activity, users can analyze historical data to understand patterns of resource usage and identify trends associated with potential security incidents. Self-auditing log files ensure that all process interactions are tracked, helping facilitate compliance and security reviews. These logs also serve as a valuable resource during incident response activities.

In addition to proactive measures, administrators must be prepared to respond to incidents involving processes. Should a breach occur, rapid identification of compromised processes is essential for limiting the impact. Understanding how to kill rogue processes or isolate compromised applications quickly can prevent unauthorized access to sensitive data and system controls. Establishing an incident response plan that outlines how to handle compromised processes while minimizing disruption to normal operations will enhance system resilience.

Finally, the nature of security in process management is rapidly evolving, requiring a commitment to continuous learning and adaptation. As new vulnerabilities emerge and threats evolve, staying updated with the latest security trends, best practices, and remediation techniques is paramount. Participating in the security community, attending relevant workshops, and regularly reviewing security policies ensure that organizations can effectively navigate the complexities of process management security as they arise.

In conclusion, the security implications of process management in Linux systems are multi-faceted, entwining permission management, resource allocation, application isolation, and incident response. By understanding these implications and establishing comprehensive security practices, administrators can protect their systems from potential threats posed by processes while maintaining operational integrity and performance. As they cultivate their processes with care, like a bonsai artist tending to their intricate creation, administrators can ensure that their environments thrive securely in the ever-changing landscape of cybersecurity challenges.

8. Dynamic Resource Allocation

8.1. Analyzing Resource Usage Patterns

Analyzing resource usage patterns is essential for optimizing Linux process management. In a typical Linux environment, processes perform various tasks and utilize system resources in differing ways. This subchapter will elaborate on how to effectively assess and respond to resource usage trends, which serves as a crucial component in maintaining system efficiency and stability.

Understanding resource usage patterns begins with monitoring and gathering data on how processes allocate resources such as CPU, memory, disk I/O, and network bandwidth. Various tools provide visibility into these areas, including 'top', 'htop', 'iotop', and 'netstat'. Utilizing these tools enables administrators to identify which processes are resource-intensive and understand their behavior over time.

To effectively analyze these patterns, it is beneficial to track resource usage trends over periods. Many monitoring tools can log resource utilization metrics, capturing snapshots at regular intervals. For instance, tools like Prometheus or Grafana can be configured to visualize resource consumption trends and generate alerts based on predefined thresholds. This ongoing assessment helps administrators detect unusual spikes in resource usage that may indicate inefficient processes or potential resource leaks.

A comprehensive analysis also necessitates understanding the normal operating parameters for processes. Establishing baseline metrics allows for effective comparisons when evaluating current resource usage. Efficiency measurements may include average CPU and memory usage under typical loads, response times for services, and I/O operations for various applications. Collecting historical data is vital for establishing these benchmarks and can be instrumental in predicting future resource needs, especially when scaling developers' applications.

Responding to resource usage patterns effectively requires a proactive approach. For instance, if a process is consistently breaching resource thresholds, it may warrant further investigation. Understanding the underlying causes of excessive resource consumption can lead to actionable steps, such as optimizing application code, revising configuration settings, or temporarily limiting competing processes to alleviate strain on resources.

In cases where processes exhibit erratic or unpredictable behavior, examining their logs can help diagnose issues. Review logs for high-usage processes to uncover potential errors or patterns that correlate with usability issues. This diligent investigation can reveal misconfigurations, memory leaks, or other problems that may be resolved through targeted interventions.

Identifying which processes contribute significantly to resource strain is incredibly beneficial. Administrators can prioritize processes based on their role in the application ecosystem and user experience. Critical services that require more dedicated resources may benefit from adjustments in priority, while less important background processes may be deprioritized or gently pruned as resource needs dictate.

Moreover, workload balancing strategies can be adopted to distribute resource loads evenly across processes. Load balancing can be implemented via scheduling adjustments, where batch jobs or intensive processes are staggered to prevent overwhelming the system. Preventing resource contention not only improves responsiveness but also enhances stability, particularly in environments with high-volume transactions or applications.

Automating responses to specific resource usage trends is another effective tactic. For instance, administrators can establish scripts to automatically adjust process priorities based on CPU utilization or to restart processes that exceed memory thresholds. Such scheduled scripts free administrators from the need to intervene manually while ensuring optimal resource distribution.

Being aware of the implications of resource usage patterns on user experience is equally crucial. Processes that slow down user applications or services can lead to frustration and operational inefficiencies. Training and communication with the user base regarding known high-resource processes or potential bottlenecks can promote understanding and collaborative problem-solving.

In conclusion, analyzing resource usage patterns is an integral function of effective process management in Linux systems. By setting up robust monitoring practices, establishing baseline parameters, responding proactively to usage trends, and considering user experiences, administrators can foster an efficient and stable environment. Engaging with data and adopting a systematic approach to understanding and acting on resource usage not only enhances performance but also elevates the overall user experience, driving productivity in a well-tuned Linux landscape. Each analysis and response contributes to a thriving process ecosystem, much like a caringly maintained bonsai that flourishes through thoughtful cultivation.

8.2. Tools for Dynamic Allocation

In the vast landscape of Linux process management, mastering the art of dynamic allocation is essential for optimizing resource utilization and ensuring system stability. The tools and methodologies available for managing resources dynamically enable administrators to keep pace with the evolving demands of users, applications, and workloads. Understanding how to leverage these tools effectively can lead to significant improvements in system efficiency and performance.

Dynamic allocation refers to the ability to adjust resource distribution —such as CPU, memory, and bandwidth—on-the-fly, based on current system demands. This adaptability is key in environments where workloads fluctuate, such as in cloud computing or multi-user systems. To implement dynamic resource management effectively, one must first analyze resource usage patterns, employ tools that facilitate dynamic allocation, automate process adjustments, and balance distribution in real-time.

Analyzing resource usage patterns involves collecting and interpreting data on how processes utilize system resources over time. Tools like 'top', 'htop', and 'sar' provide real-time insights into CPU load, memory usage, swap activity, and disk I/O, allowing administrators to identify trends and anticipate resource needs. Historical data analysis through tools like Grafana and Prometheus can uncover patterns of resource consumption, helping to project future requirements and make informed decisions about resource allocation.

Tools for dynamic allocation come in many forms, each designed to enhance the handling of resource distribution. For instance, Linux Control Groups (cgroups) allow for the grouping of processes and the application of resource limits at the group level. Administrators can configure cgroups to restrict CPU and memory usage for various processes, effectively prioritizing critical applications while preventing lower-priority processes from consuming excessive resources. Additionally, process schedulers, like the Completely Fair Scheduler (CFS) in the Linux kernel, allow for efficient management of CPU time across multiple processes, ensuring that resources are allocated dynamically based on process needs.

Automating process adjustments is another key component of dynamic allocation. Automation tools like Ansible, Puppet, or custom scripts can be employed to monitor resource consumption and make real-time changes based on predefined conditions. For example, an automated script might monitor CPU usage and dynamically adjust process priorities or even scale resources in a cloud environment. This approach not only optimizes performance but also reduces the administrative burden on system administrators.

Memory and CPU allocation strategies should be carefully crafted to align with the demands of running applications. A balanced approach to these allocations considers average load patterns, peaks in usage, and overall system capacity. By continuously monitoring these metrics and adjusting settings accordingly, administrators can ensure that memory and CPU resources are utilized efficiently, maintaining system responsiveness even under heavy loads.

As technology evolves, the future directions in resource management will likely involve enhanced machine learning algorithms and predictive analytics. These advancements will enable administrators to forecast resource demands more accurately and make proactive adjustments in real-time, further optimizing processes for efficiency.

In conclusion, the tools and methodologies for dynamic allocation in Linux are instrumental in managing resources effectively. By analyzing usage patterns, employing dynamic allocation tools, automating adjustments, and strategically balancing memory and CPU use, administrators can adapt to changing demands and ensure their systems run smoothly. Embracing these practices creates an environment where processes flourish, and resource management becomes an art form—a finely tuned craft akin to the meticulous care required to nurture a bonsai tree to perfection. With continued advancements on the horizon, the landscape of dynamic resource management in Linux systems promises exciting possibilities for enhanced efficiency and scalability.

8.3. Automating Process Adjustments

In the dynamic world of Linux process management, automating process adjustments can substantially optimize operations and improve system efficiency. Automation in this context refers to the implementation of systems and tools that allow for the dynamic modification of process settings without manual intervention. This can involve adjusting process priorities, managing resource allocations, and responding to real-time performance metrics.

A key starting point for automation is understanding the triggers for adjustments. Using monitoring tools like 'top,' 'htop,' or more sophisticated solutions such as Prometheus or Grafana, administrators can collect data on process behavior and system resource usage. These monitoring systems can be set to send alerts or automatically invoke scripts when certain thresholds are crossed, such as excessive CPU or memory usage. For instance, if a process exceeds a predetermined CPU usage level consistently, an automated script might increase its nice value to lower its priority, effectively juggling the load with minimal manual oversight.

Scripting languages like Python or Bash offer great flexibility in creating automation scripts tailored to specific environments. Admins can write scripts to monitor processes and spawn new ones, adjust resource limits on the fly, or even restart applications that fail to respond appropriately. These scripts can be scheduled using cron jobs or systemd timers to maintain continuous oversight while allowing the system to self-manage in response to real-time demands.

Another powerful automation strategy lies in leveraging orchestration tools. For instance, Kubernetes provides native support for dynamic resource allocations within containerized environments. This allows organizations to define rules on how to scale applications based on resource utilization dynamically. With features like Horizontal Pod Autoscaling, Kubernetes can automatically adjust the number of pods running an application based on CPU or memory consumption, ensuring optimal performance while minimizing wasted resources.

Automation should not only be reactive but also proactive. Incorporating predictive analysis into process management can significantly enhance automation effectiveness. Machine learning models can analyze historical resource usage data to forecast future needs, allowing administrators to preemptively allocate resources or scale applications before issues arise. This predictive approach ensures a seamless experience for users while maintaining system integrity.

Balancing automation with human oversight is crucial for effective process management. While the automated systems perform optimally in handling day-to-day fluctuations, administrators must establish clear protocols for monitoring the automated operations and intervening as necessary. This balance ensures that while automation frees up valuable time and reduces the risk of human error, it does not remove the human element necessary for nuanced decision-making, especially during complex or unprecedented situations.

Furthermore, it's essential to document automation processes thoroughly. This documentation helps in understanding the rationale behind specific adjustments made by scripts or systems and facilitates troubleshooting if a particular automation leads to unexpected consequences. Clear records allow teams to review and refine automation strategies continuously, fostering a culture of improvement and learning.

In conclusion, automating process adjustments is vital to modern Linux process management. By utilizing monitoring tools, scripting languages, orchestration technologies, and predictive analytics, system administrators can streamline operations and respond to resource demands dynamically. This proactive approach enhances system efficiency and user satisfaction while preserving the essential human oversight necessary for complex decision-making. Embracing automation marks a strategic evolution in the art of process management, allowing Linux systems to adapt seamlessly to evolving challenges and opportunities, much like a beautifully maintained bonsai trees adapt and thrive through careful cultivation.

8.4. Memory and CPU Allocation

In the increasingly complex world of Linux systems, memory and CPU allocation is a critical aspect of process management that determines the overall performance and efficiency of applications. Just as a bonsai artist orchestrates the growth of a tree by controlling its environment and resources, system administrators must skillfully allocate memory and CPU to processes, ensuring that each one receives the right amount of resources without overburdening the system.

Efficient memory allocation begins with a clear understanding of the memory hierarchy in Linux, including the distinctions between physical memory, virtual memory, and swap space. Processes utilize memory through a structured layout that includes sections such as the code segment, heap, stack, and data segment, each serving a unique purpose. Being aware of how each process allocates memory helps administrators spot inefficiencies and optimize usage. Tools like `free`, `vmstat`, and `top` provide essential insights into memory usage patterns, enabling administrators to monitor and adjust allocations proactively.

Central to effective memory management is the concept of allocation strategies. The choice between static and dynamic allocation strategies significantly influences how efficiently processes use memory. Static allocation fixes a process's memory size at compile time, which can lead to wasted resources if the allocation exceeds the actual demands. In contrast, dynamic allocation allows memory to be allocated and deallocated at runtime, which is often more efficient, particularly for processes with unpredictable memory usage. By leveraging dynamic allocation techniques—such as using `malloc` in C programming or leveraging modern programming languages' built-in garbage collection—administrators and developers can foster a more efficient memory management strategy, catering to application demands without sacrificing performance.

On the CPU front, allocating processing power to various processes involves balancing the need for responsiveness against the constraints of available CPU cycles. The Linux kernel employs a preemptive scheduling model that dynamically manages CPU time slices among competing processes. This core scheduling strategy is crucial for ensuring that CPU-intensive processes do not monopolize resources, leading to system unresponsiveness. Administrators can use priorities and the nice value settings to influence how the scheduler allocates CPU time. Processes with lower nice values receive higher priority and greater access to CPU cycles, while processes with higher values are deprioritized, ensuring a more balanced distribution of CPU resources across applications and users.

Effective CPU allocation also relies on understanding process states —how processes transition between running, sleeping, waiting, and halted states impacts how CPU cycles are allocated. Employing monitoring tools, like `top` or `htop`, administrators can visualize active and sleeping processes, identifying those that might be unnecessarily prolonging resource contention. Intelligent responses, such as dynamically adjusting process priorities or terminating stalled processes, can further improve CPU efficiency.

In modern multi-core processors, optimizing memory and CPU allocations also demands an understanding of how processes can better utilize these cores. Multi-threaded applications may benefit from being allocated across multiple cores rather than limited to a single thread executing on one core. This can significantly enhance throughput and overall performance. Tools such as `taskset` can be utilized to set processor affinity, ensuring specific processes run on designated cores to reduce context switching overhead. Additionally, with an eye toward future scalability, incorporating techniques like load balancing extends across nodes in a computer cluster, allowing even greater allocation efficiency as demands grow or fluctuate.

As technology continues to advance, the landscape of dynamic memory and CPU allocation is shifting toward automation and artificial intelligence. As systems monitor their own performance, they can self-optimize resource allocation based on actual usage patterns —eliminating reliance on manual settings and configurations. The emergence of AI-based resource management tools opens the door for even more sophisticated approaches, applying machine learning algorithms to predict peak loads and optimize resource distribution in real-time.

In conclusion, mastering memory and CPU allocation in a Linux environment is a multi-faceted endeavor that requires a blend of theoretical knowledge, practical monitoring, strategic adjustments, and ongoing adaptation to technological changes. By maintaining a proactive approach and leveraging both traditional tools and emerging technologies, system administrators can ensure that processes operate smoothly and efficiently, balancing resource distribution effectively. Just as a bonsai artist nurtures their tree into a balanced and vibrant shape, so too can administrators cultivate a responsive and high-performing Linux system through disciplined memory and CPU allocation strategies.

8.5. Future Directions in Resource Management

In the evolving landscape of Linux process management, future directions in resource management promise to shape the efficiency and scalability of systems significantly. As organizations increasingly rely on robust computing environments, understanding and leveraging emerging trends and technologies will be essential.

One of the foremost trends is the shift towards cloud computing and hybrid environments, where dynamic resource management is crucial. Cloud platforms such as AWS, Azure, and Google Cloud offer automated scaling that adjusts resources in real time based on demand. These capabilities not only enhance performance but also reduce costs by optimizing resource use. The ability to programmatically allocate and deallocate resources in response to fluctuating workloads signifies a paradigm shift in how resource allocation is approached. This trend will likely encourage Linux administrators to develop proficiency in the API-based management of processes within cloud environments, integrating traditional tools with cloud-native solutions.

Additionally, containerization is revolutionizing the way processes are managed. Technologies like Docker and Kubernetes allow processes to run in isolated environments, enabling more efficient use of system resources. The orchestration capabilities in Kubernetes, specifically, allow for automatic scaling, health checks, and the ability to manage container lifecycles dynamically. As these technologies continue to mature, administrators will need to adapt their skill sets to include container management techniques and understand the implications of orchestration on resource normalization.

Machine learning and artificial intelligence are also making their way into the realm of process management. These technologies can analyze vast amounts of data regarding resource usage patterns, identify anomalies, and even predict future resource needs. Employing machine learning algorithms to automate resource allocation decisions will not only enhance operational efficiency but will also reduce the risk of human error in process management. Future directions in resource management could see systems that intelligently allocate resources, optimizing performance without requiring manual intervention.

The rise of edge computing is another factor influencing resource management. With the proliferation of IoT devices and the need for low-latency processing, edge computing necessitates a re-evaluation of how resources are allocated across distributed systems. Linux administrators may find themselves optimizing processes based on locality—ensuring that data processing occurs as close to the source as possible. This shift will require new strategies for resource distribution that take both resource availability and latency into consideration.

Moreover, container orchestration aligns well with microservices architecture, facilitating the dynamic allocation of resources based on service needs rather than static allocations. This architectural trend emphasizes decentralized management, resilience, and scalability. Tools specifically designed for managing microservices, such as Istio for service mesh, will likely become integral in controlling and monitoring workloads across multiple services, allowing for finer control over resource management at a granular level.

As these trends unfold, security concerns surrounding resource management will require greater attention. With the complexities introduced by cloud and containerized environments, managing user permissions and ensuring process isolation will be paramount. Administrators will have to navigate the delicate balance between accessibility and security while managing processes in increasingly interconnected and interdependent systems.

Finally, the shift towards DevOps and continuous delivery methodologies emphasizes automation in process management. The future will see a greater reliance on infrastructure as code, in which resources are provisioned and managed through code rather than manual configurations. This approach not only streamlines deployments but also allows for version control and rollback capabilities

—providing a robust mechanism for managing process changes over time.

In summary, the future of Linux process management revolves around the integration of cloud computing, containerization, machine learning, edge computing, microservices architectures, and enhanced security strategies. As these trends emerge, Linux administrators must continuously adapt their skills, embracing new tools and methodologies that align with these advancements. By doing so, they will cultivate an environment capable of running efficient and scalable processes, positioning themselves and their organizations for success in an unpredictable technological landscape.

9. Handling Process Dependencies

9.1. Identifying Process Dependencies

Identifying the dependencies between processes is crucial for system integrity and performance in any Linux environment. Processes often interact with one another, relying on shared resources, libraries, and data. Understanding these relationships is fundamental for efficient management, troubleshooting, and optimization.

One of the first steps in identifying process dependencies is to utilize tools that provide visibility into running processes and their interactions. The 'ps' command, with options like 'ps -ef' or 'ps aux', produces a comprehensive list of active processes, including their parent process ID (PPID). This allows administrators to ascertain parent-child relationships within the process tree. By understanding these relationships, administrators can pinpoint which processes are responsible for spawning others, facilitating the determination of dependencies.

Another powerful tool for visualizing process dependencies is 'pstree'. This command displays the process hierarchy in a tree-like format, making it easier to see how processes are related to one another. By using 'pstree -p', the output includes process IDs, which can help in further investigating specific processes that may be causing issues or consuming excessive resources.

In more complex scenarios, administrators may turn to specialized tools like SystemTap or strace. SystemTap is a powerful scripting language and tool that enables users to probe system events and gather detailed insights into process behavior. By writing scripts that track specific processes and their interactions, administrators can uncover dependencies that might not be immediately visible. Similarly, strace allows one to trace system calls made by a process, revealing how it interacts with the underlying operating system and other processes.

Understanding the roles of shared libraries is also essential in the context of identifying dependencies. When processes load dynamic libraries, they become reliant on those libraries for functionality.

Tools like `ldd` can be used to list the shared libraries a particular executable depends on. This knowledge is vital for administrators, as missing or incompatible libraries can lead to runtime errors or unexpected behavior in processes.

In addition to these tools, processes may communicate and depend on each other through Inter-Process Communication (IPC) mechanisms, such as message queues, semaphores, or shared memory. It is essential to monitor and understand how these IPC methods are being utilized; tools like `ipcs` or `ipcmk` can help in inspecting existing message queues or shared memory segments.

Dependency management should also take into account system resources. Processes that tie together through data dependencies (for example, a web server and its backend database) should be evaluated for their resource allocation needs as well since delays or high load in one can result in cascading effects on others. Automated monitoring solutions that track resource usage can alert administrators when relevant processes are exhibiting suspicious behavior or when resource limits are approached.

By establishing clear documentation of processes and their dependencies, administrators can create a better understanding of their environment. A visual representation or a dependency map can serve as a reference for future troubleshooting and performance assessments.

In conclusion, identifying process dependencies is a vital task that requires a combination of monitoring tools, hierarchy analysis, and an understanding of system resource interaction. By using available tools effectively and documenting relationships, system administrators can optimize process management, facilitate troubleshooting, and enhance overall system performance, ensuring that their Linux environments operate smoothly and efficiently.

9.2. Resolving Dependency Conflicts

Resolving dependency conflicts in a Linux operating system is paramount for ensuring operational stability and performance. Dependency conflicts can arise when multiple processes rely on the same resources, libraries, or services, leading to inefficiencies or system failures. Effectively identifying and resolving these conflicts enables system administrators to maintain a harmonious computing environment where processes can thrive without contention.

One of the primary strategies for resolving dependency conflicts is to visualize the dependencies between processes. Utilizing tools such as `pstree` provides a clear view of parent-child relationships among processes, highlighting direct dependencies. A well-structured approach includes examining the output of `ps aux` to capture processes and their associated resource usage. This information can be laid out in tables or charts for more detailed analysis.

In multi-process environments, blocking or waiting states can indicate potential conflicts. Monitoring tools like `top` or `htop` help to easily identify when processes are stuck, indicating that dependencies may not be met. For example, a child process that is not being allocated necessary resources from a parent process could lead to timeouts or crashes. Understanding how dependencies map can provide insights into which processes might need intervention or reconfiguration to allow for smoother execution.

When conflicts are identified, adjusting process scheduling can often alleviate tension. Linux employs several scheduling algorithms in process control, which controls how CPU time is allocated to the processes. By prioritizing processes that are more critical or adjusting the nice values of less important processes, administrators can attempt to free up resources that may be causing bottlenecks. The `renice` command allows for easy adjustments to the scheduling priorities, enabling dynamic reallocation of resources based on changing demands.

If the conflicts arise due to competing processes trying to access the same resources, implementing resource control through cgroups can be effective. Cgroups allow administrators to restrict the resources allocated to specific processes, ensuring that resource contention is mitigated. By setting limits on CPU, memory, and I/O for specific processes, administrators can effectively manage dependencies without sacrificing overall system performance.

In some situations, it may be necessary to refactor processes or applications, particularly if conflicts are recurring. This can involve changing how applications are designed to interact – decoupling processes where high levels of interdependence lead to clashes. Furthermore, introducing asynchronous processing can allow processes to operate independently, thereby avoiding blocking states that contribute to conflicts.

Documentation plays a crucial role in resolving dependency conflicts as well. Keeping track of which processes depend on others, and the specific interactions—especially across critical systems—can provide a valuable reference when new issues arise. Creating and maintaining a dependency map allows for quick identification of at-risk processes when conflicts emerge and guides future decision-making about process management.

Finally, fostering a culture of collaboration and communication among team members is essential in managing dependency conflicts. Engaging developers, users, and administrators in discussions surrounding resource demands and efficiency can yield innovative solutions and minimize potential conflicts. Conducting regular reviews of resource allocations, monitoring tools, and overall system performance will empower teams to react promptly to emerging conflicts.

In conclusion, resolving dependency conflicts in Linux processes is a multi-faceted approach that requires a combination of visualization, monitoring, process adjustment, resource control, and clear documentation. By adequately identifying dependencies and conflicts, and effectively managing system resources, administrators can maintain a balanced environment where processes can coexist and function optimally, ensuring the overall health and responsiveness of the Linux system. With a systematic approach to conflict resolution, system administrators can enjoy a landscape that promotes efficiency and harmony amongst the various processes shaping the operational fabric of their environments.

9.3. Scripting for Dependency Management

Scripting for Dependency Management is a critical skill for system administrators who seek to ensure efficient operation and healthy performance of Linux environments. With the intricate web of processes and their interdependencies, the need to automate dependency management has never been greater. This subchapter delves into the strategies and techniques for effectively scripting to handle process dependencies, ultimately boosting performance, reducing manual workloads, and enhancing system stability.

To begin scripting for dependency management, administrators must first understand the nature of process relationships within the Linux environment. Processes often rely on shared resources, data files, or inter-process communication mechanisms. By documenting and analyzing these dependencies, you can create a baseline for developing automation scripts that monitor and manage these relationships.

One common approach to automating dependency management includes using shell scripts to monitor the status of processes and their dependencies. A basic script can utilize commands like ps or pgrep to check if essential services are running before starting dependent processes. A simple script might look like this:

```bash
\#!/bin/bash

\# Check if the database service is running
if ! pgrep -x "database_service" > /dev/null; then
    echo "Starting the database service..."
    systemctl start database_service
fi

\# Now start the web application after confirming the
database is running
if pgrep -x "database_service" > /dev/null; then
    echo "Starting the web application..."
    systemctl start web_application
```

```
else
    echo "Error: Database service failed to start."
fi
```

This example demonstrates a basic script that checks for a database service's status and ensures it is running before starting an associated web application. Scripts like these can help manage processes dynamically based on their dependencies, ensuring a chain reaction of correct launches without manual oversight.

When developing scripts for dependency management, leveraging scheduling tools like `cron` can be beneficial. Automating scripts to run at specific intervals or during system downtime can ensure that processes are appropriately managed without requiring administrator intervention. For example, a `cron` job can run daily to check the health of critical services and restart them if necessary, thus maintaining system resilience.

Beyond basic checks, more advanced scripts can incorporate logging mechanisms that track process states and resource usage over time. By utilizing tools such as `syslog`, administrators can capture and store critical data regarding process behavior. Incorporating error handling into the scripts allows the system to react appropriately to different situations, such as notifying the administrator via email or logging to a central repository when processes fail or exhibit unusual behavior.

Furthermore, when dealing with complex dependencies, system administrators may benefit from versioning their scripts and employing structure through version control systems like Git. This practice allows for tracking changes, collaborating with team members, and reverting to previous states should issues arise after updates.

In addition to monitoring, automation scripts can facilitate the management of process priorities. By incorporating the `renice` command into scripts, administrators can dynamically adjust the priority of a running process based on workload demands or detected issues. For example:

```
\#!/bin/bash
```

```
\# Identify high CPU consuming process and adjust its
priority
high_cpu_process=$(ps --sort=-%cpu | awk 'NR==2 {print $1}')
\# Gets PID of the process consuming most CPU
renice +5 $high_cpu_process \# Adjust priority to lower
```

This snippet identifies the process consuming the highest CPU resources and lowers its priority to allow for a more equitable distribution of resources among other critical processes.

Finally, the future of scripting for dependency management will continue to evolve with the advent of automation frameworks and tools. Technologies such as Ansible, Puppet, and Chef are increasingly used to manage process dependencies through infrastructure as code principles, allowing for sophisticated editing, deployment automation, and scaling. Learning these tools can equip administrators with enhanced capabilities to manage dependencies across their Linux environments effectively.

In conclusion, scripting for dependency management is an indispensable practice for Linux system administrators. By employing scripts to monitor process statuses, log behaviors, automate service starts, and manage priorities, administrators can streamline operations significantly while minimizing manual intervention. The ability to handle process dependencies effectively lays the groundwork for a stable, efficient, and responsive Linux environment, echoing the careful cultivation required to maintain a balanced bonsai tree. Ultimately, as administrators embrace these practices, they contribute to a process ecosystem that is resilient, adaptable, and poised for success.

9.4. Role of System Libraries

In the context of process management in Linux environments, system libraries serve as foundational components that dictate how processes operate within a defined framework. These libraries encapsulate functionalities that programs require, allowing them to perform a plethora of tasks without needing to reinvent the wheel. The role of system libraries in process management is multifaceted, influencing everything from how processes communicate to the efficiency of resource allocation.

At a fundamental level, system libraries are collections of precompiled routines that process runtime execution interfaces with system calls. These libraries provide essential functions that support process interactions with system resources, including file handling, memory management, and network communication. By abstracting these functionalities, libraries foster modular programming, enabling developers to focus on higher-level logic without delving into the intricacies of system calls.

When a process is launched, it may invoke various library functions that allow it to perform its intended tasks. For example, a web server might make use of network sockets provided by libraries such as `libc`, enabling it to accept client connections and transmit data. The efficiency of these operations directly influences how well the process performs under load. Optimizing library usage involves selecting the right libraries and understanding the system calls they make, which is vital for enhancing process efficiency and responsiveness.

Moreover, libraries allow for shared resource management across multiple processes. When different processes utilize the same library, they can share the underlying code in memory, reducing the overall footprint on system resources. This shared usage minimizes memory overhead and allows for efficient updates; when a library is enhanced or patched, all processes depending on it benefit from the improvements without needing to be individually recompiled. Therefore, selecting widely-used and optimized libraries is pivotal for performance.

However, dependencies on system libraries can also introduce challenges in process management. A library update can have cascading effects on dependent processes—if an API change leads to compatibility issues, processes relying on the previous version may fail to execute correctly. Thus, when managing processes, administrators must maintain awareness of library dependencies and ensure that their systems are running compatible versions.

For effective process management, tracking which libraries are loaded by running processes can be accomplished with tools such as `ldd`, which lists the shared libraries used by an executable. Knowing which libraries are in use provides insight into potential dependencies and helps administrators anticipate impacts due to future updates or changes.

In a dynamic environment, the versioning of libraries becomes particularly crucial. Tools like `apt`, `yum`, or `dnf` depend on package management systems to ensure that library versions are consistently managed, thus alleviating many compatibility issues that could arise from manual updates. Ensuring libraries are up-to-date and secure is imperative, as vulnerabilities often emerge in outdated libraries that threaten process integrity.

Finally, it is essential to incorporate proper error handling for scenarios where critical library calls may fail. This could involve establishing fallback mechanisms, logging errors for investigation, or alerting systems. Such preemptive measures enable administrators to maintain system reliability even when processes encounter issues related to their necessary libraries.

In conclusion, the role of system libraries in Linux process management is profound, affecting process efficiency, resource allocation, and overall system stability. By leveraging libraries effectively while being cognizant of their dependencies and impacts, system administrators can optimize process performance and preserve the integrity of their Linux environments. This relationship embodies the principle of creating a cohesive and well-functioning ecosystem, akin to nurturing a bonsai—where every element contributes harmoniously to the whole.

9.5. Monitoring Dependency Integrity

In today's hyper-connected world, where processes intertwine like branches in a dense forest, the integrity of dependencies among them becomes a crucial factor in overall system reliability. Monitoring dependency integrity refers to the practice of assessing and maintaining the health of crucial process relationships, ensuring that each process executes reliably and harmoniously. This task not only demands technical mastery of Linux systems but also requires a proactive approach to troubleshooting and resource management, frequently encapsulated in the broader context of system administration.

Understanding the role of dependencies is the first step toward effective monitoring. Each process in a Linux environment may rely on others for functionality, whether through shared libraries, inter-process communication, or a hierarchical relationship where parent processes spawn child processes. When these dependencies function well, the system operates smoothly, resembling a finely tuned orchestra. However, disruptions — be they in the form of a crashed parent process, insufficient resources, or library issues — can lead to cascading failures that ripple through the dependent processes.

One essential strategy for monitoring dependency integrity involves establishing clear visibility into the relationships among processes. Tools like `pstree` provide visual representations of process trees, illustrating parent-child relationships and highlighting which processes depend on others. Leveraging this visual information allows administrators to quickly diagnose which processes may be affected by failures within the tree.

In addition to hierarchical visualization, the use of command-line utilities such as `ps` can afford deeper insights into each process's resource utilization, shedding light on potential risks to integrity. By frequently assessing resource consumption metrics—CPU and memory usage, I/O operations, and wait states — administrators can identify processes that are not only resource-heavy but might also exhibit signs of instability.

In a scenario where a parent process becomes unresponsive or consumes extensive resources, it can jeopardize the execution of its children. This dependency chain highlights the necessity of real-time monitoring and quick remediation. Scripting automated responses, such as invoking alerts when a parent process becomes idle beyond a specific threshold or monitoring response times, ensures that administrators can preemptively address dependency issues.

Furthermore, resource management becomes critical to preserving the integrity of dependencies. By employing control groups (cgroups) or implementing priorities through the nice command, administrators can ensure that critical processes receive the necessary resources while deprioritizing less critical tasks to maintain system responsiveness. Monitoring tools can help identify which dependencies are experiencing contention, enabling timely adjustments.

Another effective technique involves establishing automated logging and alerting mechanisms. By utilizing systemd or monitoring frameworks like Zabbix or Nagios, administrators can capture and log events related to process states and transitions. Automating alerts that trigger when specific processes fail or when critical thresholds are breached aids in maintaining an awareness of dependency integrity in real time.

However, simply monitoring dependency integrity is insufficient; it must be complemented by strategic responses to issues identified. Engaging in proactive troubleshooting plays an essential role when potential conflicts arise. Analyzing logs, reviewing resource settings, and understanding application interdependencies can reveal whether dependency issues were caused by application bugs, configuration errors, or resource-finding priorities.

Documenting dependency relationships, system behaviors, and resolutions found during monitoring can aid future troubleshooting efforts, fostering an environment of continual improvement. By creating detailed reports that capture process relationships, typical behaviors, and any issues observed over time, administrators build an invaluable knowledge base that can guide future process management decisions.

In conclusion, monitoring dependency integrity is an essential practice for Linux system administrators looking to maintain stable and resilient environments. By cultivating an understanding of process relationships, employing real-time resource monitoring, establishing automated alerts, and engaging in proactive troubleshooting, administrators can ensure that processes interact harmoniously. This comprehensive approach to managing process dependencies preserves system integrity and ultimately contributes to a more robust Linux environment capable of responding efficiently to challenges. As you cultivate your system akin to nurturing a bonsai, you ensure each process remains vital and integrated within the intricate ecosystem of your Linux environment.

10. Performance Monitoring and Tuning

10.1. Benchmarking Process Performance

As the field of Linux process management continues to evolve, benchmarking process performance emerges as a key area of focus. Effective benchmarking involves creating a set of performance metrics that enable system administrators to assess how various processes within their systems are performing relative to one another and to established performance baselines. This benchmarking allows for effective decision-making and management of processes, leading to more responsive systems.

Begin the benchmarking process by identifying the specific metrics that are important for assessing process performance. These can include CPU usage, memory consumption, disk I/O operations, and response times for processes. The aim is to quantify these metrics to provide a clear picture of performance. Selecting suitable benchmarks tailored to your system's particular workload is essential, as this will provide actionable insights that can lead to improvements.

One effective tool for benchmarking is the `time` command, which allows administrators to measure how long a particular process runs and the CPU time it consumes. For example, running a command like `time my_process` will yield an output summarizing the real (wall-clock) time taken, user CPU time, and system CPU time. This data can then be aggregated for multiple runs to produce a more reliable benchmark, aiding in the understanding of how changes in configurations or code affect performance.

Another useful tool for more comprehensive benchmarking is `sysbench`, which enables administrators to perform various benchmarks on CPU, memory, file I/O, and multi-threaded workloads. Through a series of tests, `sysbench` can reveal how processes behave under load, and identify processes that may become bottlenecks as system demands grow. Administrators can generate reports detailing various workloads, allowing comparisons to be made over time or against different configurations.

For memory benchmarking, tools such as `memtester` can help assess how well processes manage available memory by measuring performance under various stress conditions. This can expose potential issues related to memory allocation, leaks, and fragmentation—critical insights that can facilitate process optimizations.

Network performance benchmarking tools such as `iperf` can also play an essential role in evaluating how processes that rely on network resources perform under different conditions. By simulating various network scenarios, administrators can assess how well processes handle data transmission, revealing any inefficiencies or bottlenecks arising from network interactions.

It is crucial to establish baselines against which new data can be compared. Periodically running benchmarks and evaluating how performance changes over time can help identify trends and unexpected behavior in process performance. This data serves as a foundational reference point for future assessments and can guide decision-making and resource allocation strategies.

Incorporating benchmarking results into an analysis of overall system performance can lead to insightful discovery. For instance, if a particular application consistently shows poor CPU performance during benchmarking, it may merit further investigation. Tools like `perf` provide in-depth insights on where CPU cycles are being spent and can highlight potential optimizations in the application's execution path.

Once potential performance issues are identified through benchmarking, the next step is to implement tuned configurations based on these insights. This may involve optimizing process settings, allocating resources more effectively, or modifying workloads. Once changes have been made, re-benchmarking ensures an iterative approach, providing validation of performance improvements or the need for further adjustments.

In conclusion, benchmarking process performance is an essential practice for maintaining optimum functioning in Linux systems. By systematically measuring relevant performance metrics, aggregating data over time, and making informed decisions, administrators can fine-tune processes, enhance responsiveness, and ultimately foster an efficient and resilient operating environment. Much like maintaining a flourishing bonsai tree where meticulous care leads to a vibrant and well-balanced aesthetic, rigorous benchmarking and resulting optimizations create a cohesive and responsive Linux system ready to meet the demands of its users and applications alike.

10.2. Identifying Performance Bottlenecks

Identifying performance bottlenecks in a Linux environment is essential for maintaining system efficiency and responsiveness. Performance bottlenecks can occur at various levels and be caused by multiple factors, including CPU constraints, memory limitations, high I/O wait times, and inefficient networking. As system administrators navigate the complexities of process management, recognizing these bottlenecks early on aids in optimizing resource allocation and overall system performance.

The first step in identifying performance bottlenecks is thorough monitoring. Utilizing tools such as 'top', 'htop', or 'vmstat', administrators can obtain real-time insights into CPU utilization, memory usage, and process efficiency. These monitoring tools display vital metrics such as load averages, CPU usage per process, memory consumption, and swap usage. By observing these metrics continuously, you can quickly identify processes that either consume excessive resources or experience long wait times, which may indicate a performance bottleneck.

In particular, a high CPU load can hint at processes struggling to get their tasks done efficiently. If the load average remains consistently above the number of CPU cores, it signals that there are more processes ready to run than the CPU can handle simultaneously, indicating potential throttling issues. Conversely, if CPU usage appears low but processes are slow to respond, it may point to other issues like I/O wait times or blocked processes due to dependencies.

Memory-related bottlenecks can occur when processes consume excessive amounts of RAM, forcing the system to utilize swap space. Monitoring tools reveal if high memory usage correlates with performance degradation, particularly if swapping is evident. A common indicator of a memory bottleneck is when the system starts to "thrash," meaning it spends more time swapping data in and out of memory than executing processes. Identifying processes that occupy high memory levels enables you to make informed decisions about potential process terminations, optimizations, or firmware updates.

Input/Output operations are another area to monitor closely for performance bottlenecks. Tools like 'iostat' or 'iotop' can help identify disk performance issues. If a process is caught in a long I/O wait time, it'll likely be a bottleneck affecting the overall system performance, especially in data-intensive applications, such as databases. Analyzing I/O operations and identifying which processes are heavily involved can illuminate the root cause and guide you in making appropriate adjustments, such as reordering workloads or implementing more efficient data processing methods.

Networking performance is equally important, especially in server environments where latency and throughput impact user experience. Tools like 'iftop' and 'netstat' can provide insights into network usage by showing which processes are consuming bandwidth. A sudden spike in network traffic can lead to congestion and slow responses; identifying the offending processes allows you to mitigate these issues.

After identifying these bottlenecks, the next step is implementing optimization strategies. Administrators can tweak process priorities using the nice command, allowing resource allocation to more critical processes while de-prioritizing those less impactful on system performance. Additionally, evaluating and potentially reallocating hardware resources or implementing load balancing techniques can further alleviate bottlenecks.

Another strategy could involve optimizing application configurations or upgrading system hardware to meet performance needs. For instance, adding more RAM, utilizing SSDs for faster I/O operations, or redistributing workloads effectively can greatly reduce the likelihood of future performance bottlenecks.

Once adjustments have been made, continuous monitoring is essential. Regular assessment of system metrics ensures that performance improvements are sustained over time and allows for rapid responses to newly emerging bottlenecks.

In conclusion, identifying performance bottlenecks involves vigilant monitoring, understanding key system metrics, and implementing targeted strategies for optimization. By regularly evaluating CPU, memory, I/O, and network performance, administrators can maintain responsive and efficient Linux environments. This proactive approach mirrors the careful cultivation of a bonsai tree, where attention to detail and timely interventions create a flourishing ecosystem. Through diligent identification and resolution of bottlenecks, administrators can foster an environment where processes operate smoothly, contributing to overall system health and user satisfaction.

10.3. Optimizing CPU Utilization

Optimizing CPU utilization is a crucial aspect of maintaining a high-performing Linux system, especially in environments where multiple processes are fought to share limited CPU resources. Proper CPU utilization ensures that processes execute efficiently, leading to improved response times and overall system stability. This subchapter delves into various techniques and best practices for optimizing CPU utilization, guiding administrators toward achieving a finely-tuned system.

To begin with, it is essential to understand how the Linux kernel schedules processes for execution. The Linux kernel employs several scheduling algorithms to ensure that processes receive CPU time according to their priority and resource needs. The Completely Fair Scheduler (CFS) is the default algorithm used in modern Linux kernels, and it spreads CPU time fairly among all runnable processes. Understanding the workings of CFS allows administrators to make informed decisions on how to manipulate process priorities effectively.

One effective technique for optimizing CPU utilization is adjusting process priorities using the `nice` and `renice` commands. The `nice` command allows you to set a priority value when launching a new process, while `renice` enables you to change the priority of an already running process. Lowering the nice value (and thus increasing priority) of critical processes ensures they receive adequate CPU time, preventing starvation in low-priority processes. Conversely, it is equally important to identify processes that are unnecessarily hogging CPU time and lower their priority. Monitoring tools like `top` or `htop` can provide visibility into CPU usage, allowing administrators to quickly spot processes that require intervention.

Additionally, utilizing CPU affinity can further optimize CPU utilization, especially in multi-core environments. CPU affinity defines the specific CPUs or cores on which a process is allowed to run. By binding processes to particular cores using the `taskset` command, you can reduce context switching overhead and improve cache usage. This technique is particularly beneficial for applications that are sensitive to latency or those requiring high levels of performance, such as databases or real-time analytical workloads.

Reducing the overall number of runnable processes at any given time can also help optimize CPU utilization. Implementing load balancing strategies across processes and servers can prevent any single CPU from becoming a bottleneck. In cloud environments or distributed systems, distributing job workloads dynamically based on resource availability can maximize CPU efficiency while maintaining responsiveness.

Monitoring and analyzing CPU performance can provide additional insights to drive optimizations. Tools like `mpstat`, `pidstat`, and `vmstat` can be employed to gather detailed metrics on CPU utilization over time. These tools allow you to assess CPU load across multiple cores, analyze CPU wait times, and observe system activity—all of which can help you pinpoint resources that may need to be adjusted for improved performance.

Beyond process management, optimizing the code and resource management of applications contributes significantly to CPU utilization. Profiling applications to identify bottlenecks and inefficient algorithms can lead to performance improvements. Tools such as gprof or perf can be used to analyze CPU usage at the function level, allowing developers to pinpoint hotspots and optimize resource usage within the application itself.

When tuning processes, it is essential to document changes and monitor the resulting performance impact. This documentation provides a reference for future optimizations and can assist in understanding process behaviors reaction to alterations in workloads or system configuration. Regular baseline benchmarking of CPU performance before and after adjustments allows administrators to verify the efficacy of tuning efforts systematically.

Another important aspect is to implement proactive monitoring and alert systems. Configure alerts that notify administrators if CPU utilization surpasses certain thresholds—this can help in preemptively tackling performance degradations before they impact users significantly. Similarly, setting automated responses to high CPU loads, like temporarily adjusting process priorities or scaling resources in cloud systems, can create a more resilient operational posture.

Lastly, when dealing with multiple users or applications, communication plays a vital role in ensuring CPU optimization. Engaging with users regarding their resource needs and maintaining transparency about resource allocation decisions fosters collaboration. It helps ensure that critical applications receive the attention they need while providing users with insights into any performance issues that may arise.

In summary, optimizing CPU utilization involves a multi-faceted approach that combines process priority adjustments, CPU affinity management, monitoring, resource distribution strategies, and application profiling. By understanding the underlying principles of CPU scheduling in Linux and employing these techniques diligently, administrators can ensure a balanced and efficient environment for all processes. This proactive approach not only enhances performance but also contributes to system stability and responsiveness, echoing the precision and care involved in nurturing a beautifully cultivated bonsai. Ultimately, an optimized CPU leads to a harmonious process ecosystem that successfully meets user demands and organizational goals alike.

10.4. Managing Memory Swaps

Managing memory swaps is a fundamental aspect of ensuring a responsive and efficient Linux environment, particularly in systems where memory resources are limited. When physical RAM is depleted, the Linux kernel utilizes swap space—essentially a designated area on disk—to handle excess memory demands. However, improper management of this swap space can lead to decreased performance, increased latency, and a sluggish user experience. Administrators must understand how to effectively manage memory swapping to optimize resource utilization and maintain system integrity.

To begin managing memory swaps effectively, it is crucial to understand how swapping works in Linux. When a process requires more memory than is physically available, the kernel looks for inactive pages of memory to move to swap space, freeing up RAM for active processes. This process, known as paging, can be beneficial for keeping critical applications running. However, frequent swapping can cause what's known as "thrashing," where the system spends more time swapping pages in and out of memory than executing processes, severely impacting performance.

One of the first steps in managing memory swaps involves monitoring swap usage. Administrators can utilize commands such as `free -h`, which displays the total, used, and available memory and swap space, providing a snapshot of the current memory situation. Alternatively, the command `swapon -s` provides a summary view of all configured swap spaces. This knowledge allows administrators to gauge whether the swap space is being utilized effectively or if modifications are needed.

The swappiness parameter is particularly important when it comes to managing memory swapping. This kernel parameter (ranging from 0 to 100) controls the tendency of the kernel to swap memory pages. A lower value (e.g., 10) will cause the kernel to prioritize keeping processes in RAM, only swapping out pages when absolutely necessary, while a higher value (e.g., 80) will encourage more aggressive swapping. Adjusting the swappiness value can have a significant impact on system responsiveness. For instance, on a desktop environment, you might want to keep swappiness low to ensure smooth performance, whereas on a server handling large data processing tasks, a higher value may be appropriate to manage workloads effectively.

To adjust the swappiness value temporarily, an administrator might use the sysctl command as follows:

```
sudo sysctl vm.swappiness=10
```

To make the change permanent, the swappiness value can be added or edited in the /etc/sysctl.conf file. It's important to understand that finding the right balance for swappiness requires testing and tuning, as each system may have unique usage patterns.

Another technique to manage memory effectively is to size the swap space appropriately. As a rule of thumb, many suggest having swap space equal to 1 to 2 times the amount of physical RAM, depending on system use cases. For systems with large amounts of RAM, such as those used for heavy workloads, the required swap space may be less than the double RAM guideline. Conversely, systems dedicated to specific heavy applications may benefit from larger swap allocations. This strategy ensures that there is enough swap space available to accommodate memory demands without excessive reliance on disk paging.

In certain situations, administrators may wish to use `swapoff` to deactivate specific swap spaces for troubleshooting or performance tuning. However, care must be taken when adjusting swap usage while processes are running, as this could lead to instability or performance degradation if memory demands exceed available resources.

In addition to monitoring and adjusting swap usage, administrators should consider the implications of using swap partitions versus swap files. While both can be used effectively, there may be performance differences based on the specific use case and system configurations. Swap files, for example, can provide more flexibility since they can be resized easily and do not require a dedicated partition. In contrast, swap partitions can offer slightly better performance due to contiguous disk space allocation.

In scenarios where applications consistently require excessive memory, considering application optimizations or resource allocation adjustments may also be necessary. This could involve fine-tuning application settings to reduce memory usage or employing load balancing techniques to distribute processes more efficiently.

Another important aspect of managing memory swaps is maintaining awareness of how swap space impacts performance under varying load conditions. Performance monitoring tools like `vmstat`, `iotop`, and 'sar' can provide insights into memory utilization, swapping activity, and system load. These insights aid administrators in assessing whether adjustments to swapping strategies are needed.

In conclusion, managing memory swaps is a vital function for system administrators aiming to keep their Linux environments responsive and efficient. By understanding the mechanisms of swapping, monitoring swap usage, adjusting the swappiness parameter, sizing swap space appropriately, and continuously analyzing performance under load, administrators can maintain optimal memory management practices. This comprehensive approach not only helps in maximizing performance but ultimately leads to users enjoying a fluid experience —much like a well-maintained bonsai tree that flourishes through careful attention to its growth and resource needs. By honing memory swap management skills, administrators ensure that their Linux systems effectively balance system performance with resource demands, paving the way for stability and efficiency in a dynamic computing landscape.

10.5. Network Impact on Process Efficiency

As system administration continues to evolve in the realms of technology and user demands, the management of processes in Linux becomes increasingly intricate. One of the most significant areas impacting process efficiency is networking. This section delves into the profound influence networking has on the performance of processes within a Linux system and outlines key strategies for enhancing networking to optimize overall process performance.

At the outset, understanding how processes communicate over the network is vital. Many applications on a Linux system rely on network communications to function effectively, ranging from web servers responding to client requests to databases processing queries. This means that any inefficiencies or bottlenecks in the network can directly impact the performance of these processes. Monitoring network usage becomes crucial in identifying these potential pitfalls; tools like `iftop`, `nload`, and `iperf` provide real-time insights into network bandwidth utilization, enabling administrators to spot anomalies and adjust accordingly.

Network latency is another critical factor affecting process efficiency. High latency can arise from various issues, including poor network configuration, bandwidth limitations, or excessive load on the network itself. When processes experience delays in transmitting or receiving data, it can lead to timeouts, reduced responsiveness, and an overall decline in user satisfaction. By employing diagnostics tools such as `ping` and `traceroute`, administrators can pinpoint the sources of latency, allowing for targeted modifications—whether that be optimizing routing paths, upgrading hardware, or adjusting quality of service settings to prioritize critical traffic.

When dealing with processes that depend heavily on network interactions, it's advisable to implement caching strategies. Caches reduce the need to frequently retrieve the same data over the network, thus optimizing performance. For instance, utilizing a caching server or implementing a local cache within the application can significantly decrease network load and latency. By using tools such as Varnish or Redis, administrators can offload repeated queries and deliver faster responses, leading to improved efficiency for dependent processes.

Furthermore, as applications grow in complexity and scale, deploying load balancers becomes essential for distributing network traffic evenly across multiple processes. Load balancing helps ensure that no single process becomes overloaded with requests, promoting a more stable performance across the entire system. Techniques such as round-robin, least connections, or IP hash can be employed depending on the use case to optimize network traffic for distributed applications. Additionally, integrating tools like HAProxy or Nginx can enhance resilience and efficiency in managing network requests.

Security implications also come into play when considering networking's impact on process efficiency. Processes communicating over the network can be susceptible to various types of attacks, such as DDoS, data interception, and unauthorized access. Ensuring that processes implement secure communications protocols—such as TLS/SSL encryption—facilitates data integrity while also maintaining a focus on performance. Minimizing the overhead introduced by encryption through proper configurations and using efficient cipher suites can provide effective protection while preserving speed.

As system architectures evolve toward microservices and containerization, network management will take on new dimensions. Containerized processes may need to communicate across different hosts or environments, which can introduce additional challenges. Using tools like Kubernetes can help manage service discovery, routing, and load balancing between microservices efficiently, ensuring that networking remains a robust aspect of process performance.

Finally, administrators should adopt a proactive attitude when it comes to monitoring and adjusting networking configurations. Setting up alerting mechanisms that respond to network thresholds provides early indications of potential issues that could impact process performance. Regular audits of network performance metrics enable administrators to maintain a fine balance between resource allocation and user needs, ensuring a smooth operation across the system.

In conclusion, networking plays a fundamental role in the efficiency of processes within Linux systems. By utilizing monitoring tools, implementing caching strategies, deploying load balancers, prioritizing security, and adapting to new architectures, system administrators can significantly enhance network performance, leading to improved process efficiency. This undertaking forms an essential part of maintaining a responsive environment that meets the demands of users and applications alike, much like a carefully coordinated network of branches in a well-tended bonsai tree, each contributing to the harmony of the entire system.

11. Handling Multi-Core and Multi-Threaded Processors

11.1. Multitasking and Process Scheduling

In the realm of multitasking operating systems, Linux exemplifies effective process scheduling, allowing multiple processes to execute concurrently while sharing limited resources. This subchapter explores the complexities of multitasking and process scheduling within a Linux environment, emphasizing their critical role in maintaining system performance and workflow efficiency.

At the heart of multitasking is the Linux kernel's scheduling mechanism, which determines the order and priority in which processes receive CPU time. The kernel utilizes scheduling algorithms to manage the allocation of CPU resources, balancing the needs of various running processes while striving to maintain responsiveness and stability. The scheduler operates under the principle of preemptive multitasking, meaning that higher-priority processes can interrupt lower-priority processes to ensure timely execution. This approach allows the operating system to prioritize time-sensitive tasks while still managing resources for concurrent background processes.

Linux employs several scheduling algorithms, with the Completely Fair Scheduler (CFS) being the default in many modern kernels. CFS aims to provide fair and equitable CPU time allocation among processes, ensuring no single task monopolizes CPU resources. To achieve this fairness, CFS maintains a red-black tree data structure representing runnable processes sorted by their virtual runtime. By calculating an equal share of CPU time based on each process's need, CFS dynamically adjusts process priorities as CPU time is allocated.

However, while the CFS scheduler performs admirably in most scenarios, fine-tuning scheduling parameters can significantly enhance performance in specific workloads. The Linux kernel provides mechanisms for adjusting process priorities through the `nice` and `renice` commands. The `nice` command allows users to set the initial priority when starting a new process, while `renice` enables the adjustment of priorities for running processes. By leveraging these commands, administrators can optimize critical system processes, ensuring they receive the necessary CPU cycles without adversely impacting overall system performance.

Latency sensitivity is another vital consideration in multitasking and process scheduling within Linux. Some applications, such as real-time systems or interactive graphical applications, require immediate responsiveness to user input. For these types of applications, the real-time scheduling classes provided by Linux—RT (real-time) and FIFO (first-in-first-out) scheduling—offer enhanced priority control. By utilizing these scheduling classes, critical processes can be granted immediate access to CPU resources, minimizing delays and ensuring a responsive user experience.

While CPU scheduling determines which processes receive time on the CPU, it is essential to recognize the importance of memory and I/O considerations in a multitasking environment. High memory usage or excessive disk I/O on specific tasks can lead to bottlenecks, adversely impacting performance. Tools like top, iotop, and vmstat provide real-time insights into memory usage and I/O operations, enabling administrators to pinpoint problematic processes and optimize their resource consumption.

In the context of multitasking, managing process states also plays a vital role. Processes can exist in various states—running, waiting, sleeping, or stopped—and effective scheduling must consider the implications of these states. For example, a process in a waiting state due to I/O operations will yield its CPU time to other runnable processes. Understanding how processes transition between states helps administrators determine when to reinstate or prioritize certain tasks to maintain a balanced workflow.

As systems grow more complex and workloads evolve, automation becomes increasingly important in multitasking environments. Automated monitoring tools can observe process performance and resource utilization, generating alerts when specific conditions are met—such as CPU usage exceeding certain thresholds. Employing scripts that automate process adjustments based on observed trends enhances system resilience and responsiveness, allowing the scheduler to function more efficiently under varying conditions.

Furthermore, with the increasing adoption of multi-core processors, the implications of multitasking extend into multi-threading and process distribution across cores. The Linux kernel is designed to take advantage of multi-core architectures, enabling the scheduler to distribute processes across available cores effectively. This architecture boosts system throughput and responsiveness, making it essential for administrators to allocate processes intelligently and understand the nuances of effective thread management.

In conclusion, multitasking and process scheduling are essential components of Linux process management, enabling efficient resource allocation and prioritization in multi-user environments. By mastering the intricacies of scheduling algorithms, fine-tuning process priorities, managing memory and I/O interactions, and employing automation techniques, administrators can cultivate a responsive and efficient system. This meticulous approach ensures that processes operate seamlessly, addressing users' demands while maintaining overall system integrity—much like tending to a bonsai, where careful attention fosters balance and vitality within the intricate ecosystem of processes.

11.2. Adapting to Multi-Core Architectures

In the rapidly evolving realm of technology, adapting to multi-core architectures stands as both a challenge and an opportunity for Linux process management. Multi-core systems offer the promise of enhanced performance, increased efficiency, and the potential for real-time processing that single-core systems simply cannot achieve. As systems leverage multiple processing units, the ability to optimally assign and manage processes across these cores becomes paramount. This subchapter will explore the strategies and best practices for adapting processes in a Linux environment to exploit the power of multi-core architectures.

A fundamental aspect of adapting to multi-core architectures is understanding how the Linux kernel manages process scheduling for multiple cores. In a multi-core system, the kernel must efficiently allocate CPU time among all available cores while minimizing context switching. Context switching—the process by which the CPU switches from one process to another—can introduce latency and reduce overall system performance if it occurs too frequently. Thus, administrators need to ensure that processes are assigned appropriately to leverage the full capabilities of the available cores.

The Linux kernel employs scheduling policies, such as Completely Fair Scheduler (CFS), to ascertain which process gets CPU time and when. CFS aims to provide fair scheduling by managing the distribution of time slices among processes based on the number of cores available. By assessing the virtual runtime of each process, CFS strives to equalize the CPU time allocated to each one, which becomes especially critical in systems tipping toward high loads.

An effective approach to adapting processes is to utilize CPU affinity. CPU affinity allows administrators to assign specific processes to designated CPU cores. By binding a process to a particular core, the operating system reduces the overhead associated with moving the process between cores, which can lead to better cache performance and reduced latency. The `taskset` command is useful for setting CPU affinity:

```
taskset -c 0,2 my_process
```

This command binds `my_process` to cores 0 and 2, ensuring that it utilizes CPU resources without the overhead of context switching across all available cores.

Another critical element of adapting to multi-core architectures is the optimization of multi-threaded applications. Multi-threaded processes can take full advantage of multiple cores, allowing different threads to run concurrently, thus increasing efficiency. Properly implementing threading requires an understanding of concurrency control mechanisms, such as mutexes and semaphores, to prevent race conditions and ensure data integrity without negating the benefits of multi-core processing.

Employing thread pools can also enhance performance in multi-threaded applications. A thread pool maintains a limited number of threads that are reused for executing tasks, rather than constantly creating and destroying threads. This leads to lower overhead and improves throughput since threads can be executed without the cost of frequent setup.

In the context of networked applications, leveraging asynchronous I/O operations allows processes to continue executing while waiting for I/O operations to complete, freeing up CPU resources for other tasks. When combined with multi-threading, this enables the efficient handling of numerous connections or requests, which is particularly advantageous for web servers and databases.

It's equally important to examine how processes interact with shared resources in a multi-core architecture. Resource contention can emerge when multiple processes vie for access to the same data or I/O paths, leading to performance degradation. Tools like `perf`, `strace`, or `iotop` can help administrators identify performance bottlenecks arising from contention issues. Once identified, administrators may consider implementing changes to the resource allocation strategies, using control groups (cgroups) to regulate resource limits and scheduling priorities that align with the processes' demands.

The advent of virtualization technologies has also influenced how processes are managed in multi-core architectures. Virtual machines (VMs) can be configured to share multi-core resources effectively, allowing each VM to allocate underlying cores based on its workload. Techniques such as load balancing across virtual machines can amplify resource availability, enabling optimal CPU utilization.

In terms of automation, utilizing orchestration tools like Kubernetes can greatly simplify process management on multi-core systems. Kubernetes excels at dynamically allocating resources based on demand, ensuring that workloads are distributed evenly across available nodes.

By leveraging these orchestration platforms, administrators can automate the adaptation of processes according to real-time conditions, significantly improving efficiency.

In conclusion, adapting to multi-core architectures in Linux requires a combination of scheduling strategies, CPU affinity management, multi-threading optimization, resource contention mitigation, and leveraging orchestration tools. By embracing these approaches, administrators can harness the full potential of multi-core systems, fostering a responsive and efficient environment that meets user and application demands seamlessly. Just as skilled artisans cultivate their work with precision and care, so too must Linux administrators sculpt their processes for the powerful landscapes of multi-core architectures—ensuring that the system thrives and excels in performance.

11.3. Optimizing Concurrency

Optimizing concurrency in Linux process management entails maximizing the efficiency of processes that run simultaneously, particularly taking advantage of multi-core architectures and the inherent multitasking capabilities of the operating system. As systems grow in complexity and the demands on CPU and memory resources increase, mastering concurrency becomes essential for ensuring that processes are responsive, efficient, and capable of handling simultaneous tasks effectively.

One of the foundational aspects of optimizing concurrency is understanding the nature of context switching. Context switching occurs when the operating system suspends one process to resume another, thereby conserving CPU resources by allowing multiple processes to share a single CPU core. While context switching is necessary for multitasking, it does incur overhead that can impact performance. Minimizing unnecessary context switches is a critical step in enhancing concurrency. This can be achieved by favoring long-running processes that keep the CPU busy and reducing the number of short-lived processes that quickly interrupt the scheduler.

Utilizing appropriate scheduling policies is vital in optimizing concurrency. Linux employs the Completely Fair Scheduler (CFS) by default, which promotes fairness in scheduling CPU time among processes. However, users may find enhanced performance by leveraging real-time scheduling policies for processes requiring immediate responsiveness, particularly in interactive applications or real-time systems. Configuring process priorities intelligently using `nice` and `renice` commands allows administrators to prioritize critical tasks, ensuring they have sufficient processing time while still allowing other tasks to run seamlessly.

Threading plays a crucial role in optimizing concurrency as well. In multi-threaded applications, multiple threads can execute concurrently, utilizing multiple CPU cores effectively. By designing applications to be multi-threaded, developers can achieve performance gains by sharing resources and parallelizing tasks. Proper management of threading also requires effective synchronization mechanisms, such as mutexes and semaphores, to ensure data consistency across shared resources and prevent race conditions that can impede performance.

In addition to threading, process affinity is another important consideration in optimizing concurrency. By binding processes or threads to specific CPU cores using the `taskset` command, administrators can reduce cache misses and improve performance. Maintaining process affinity prevents frequent context switching, allowing processes to benefit from CPU caches effectively. This technique is particularly useful in scenarios where processes need to maintain high throughput and low latency, such as in data-intensive applications.

Monitoring tools play a significant role in optimizing concurrency. Using utilities like `htop`, `perf`, or `gprof`, administrators can gain insights into how processes utilize CPU and memory resources in real-time. Identifying processes that consume excessive resources or exhibit poor concurrency patterns can guide mitigation strategies, such as process termination, resource allocation adjustments, or code optimizations.

As systems increasingly adopt containerization and virtualization, optimizing concurrency involves ensuring that applications can operate efficiently within contained environments. Orchestration tools like Kubernetes facilitate the dynamic allocation of resources based on workload demands, enabling smooth scaling while optimizing concurrent processes. Building applications with microservices architecture allows independent scaling and management of service dependencies, which significantly enhances overall concurrency and system performance.

Finally, preparing for the future means keeping an eye on emerging technologies and trends in process optimization. As artificial intelligence and machine learning evolve, their incorporation into process management can lead to smarter resource allocation strategies and optimization techniques guided by predictive analytics. Administering systems that adapt to workload changes automatically can vastly enhance the efficiency of resource utilization and process handling, positioning organizations to thrive in an ever-competitive landscape.

In summary, optimizing concurrency in Linux requires a multi-faceted approach combining effective scheduling, process affinity management, multi-threading, and vigilant resource monitoring. By focusing on minimizing context switching, prioritizing critical processes, leveraging multi-threaded applications, and utilizing container orchestration, system administrators can achieve enhanced process efficiency. As technology progresses, embracing new tools and methodologies for concurrency management will lead to systems that are agile, responsive, and capable of delivering exceptional performance across the spectrum of tasks demanded by modern workloads.

11.4. Threading in Modern Process Architecture

Threading in Modern Process Architecture represents a pivotal advancement in the way processes are designed and executed in contemporary computing environments. In the landscape of system administration, understanding how threading interfaces with modern architecture is essential for optimizing performance, enhancing resource utilization, and ensuring effective concurrency. This section delves into the core principles of threading within process architecture, its impact on performance, and the implications for systems design and application development.

At the heart of modern process architecture is the ability to leverage threading for improved multitasking and parallel execution of tasks. Unlike traditional single-threaded processes, multi-threading allows programs to run multiple threads concurrently, enabling them to perform multiple operations simultaneously. This parallelism can lead to significant performance gains, particularly in environments where tasks can be distributed, such as web servers handling numerous client requests or data processing workloads requiring simultaneous computations.

Threading operates under the principle of shared resources, which means that threads within a process share the same memory space, allowing for fast and efficient communication. This shared memory model enhances performance significantly, as threads do not require separate memory allocation for each task, reducing overhead. However, this advantage necessitates careful design to avoid race conditions, where multiple threads simultaneously attempt to read or write shared data, potentially leading to data inconsistencies or corruption.

Developing thread-safe applications involves implementing synchronization mechanisms such as mutexes, semaphores, and condition variables. These tools allow developers to control access to shared data structures and ensure that only one thread can modify a given resource at a time. In modern process architecture, the incorrect handling of synchronization can lead to deadlocks, where threads become stuck waiting for each other to release resources, severely impacting application performance.

In the context of modern architectures that include multi-core processors, the benefits of threading become even more pronounced. Multi-core systems are designed to execute multiple threads in parallel, truly maximizing CPU utilization. System architects and developers need to consider load balancing to ensure threads are distributed across cores effectively. Thread affinity, or binding threads to specific cores, can help optimize cache usage and minimize latency. Tools like `taskset` provide administrators with the ability to control thread placement on CPUs, enhancing overall performance and responsiveness.

The concept of microservices architecture introduces another layer of complexity to the threading paradigm. In microservices, applications are constructed as a collection of loosely coupled services, each responsible for a specific function. This architecture allows for independent scaling and deployment of services, often employing threading to handle concurrent requests and background tasks efficiently. Managing inter-service communication—whether through APIs or message queues—requires careful consideration of threading and resource use to ensure that performance remains optimal across the distributed components.

Emerging technologies such as containerization also influence threading in modern process architecture. Containers like Docker encapsulate applications and their dependencies, allowing for efficient scaling and resource management. Threaded applications running within containers must be designed with resource constraints in mind, as containers share the underlying host OS's kernel and resources. Administrators must monitor and control resource allocations through cgroups to ascertain that containerized processes meet performance standards without adversely affecting one another.

In terms of programming languages, many modern languages provide robust support for threading and concurrent programming models. Languages such as Java, Go, and Rust offer built-in concurrency features that simplify the development of multi-threaded applications. Understanding how to leverage these models effectively is essential for optimizing performance in contemporary architectures. Incorporating asynchronous programming patterns and frameworks can further aid in designing responsive, concurrent applications, reducing the complexity inherent in traditional multi-threading models.

Performance benchmarking plays a vital role in evaluating the efficiency of threaded applications. Utilizing tools such as `perf`, `gprof`, or application-specific profilers allows developers to identify bottlenecks and ensure that threading constructs are optimized for the desired workload. Regular performance assessments enable continuous improvement and adaptation to changing demands and user expectations.

In conclusion, Threading in Modern Process Architecture encapsulates the evolution of how processes are structured and executed in contemporary computing environments. By leveraging threading, applications can harness the power of multi-core architectures, optimize resource utilization, and enhance responsiveness to user demands. However, the advantages of threading come with complexities that require careful design, synchronization, and monitoring. As the landscape of computing progresses, mastering threading in process architecture will become increasingly vital for administrators and developers looking to build performance-driven applications that meet the demands of an evolving digital landscape.

11.5. Real-Time Process Management

In the realm of system administration, real-time process management becomes a crucial component of ensuring efficiency and responsiveness within a Linux environment. As each process competes for system resources, managing them effectively in real-time allows administrators to maintain optimal performance levels and leverage system capabilities to their fullest.

Real-time process management involves dynamically assessing and adjusting the behavior of running processes based on their resource needs, performance metrics, and system conditions. This approach not only facilitates timely responses to resource demands but also helps to prevent bottlenecks and performance degradation that can impact overall system stability.

To begin with, effective real-time process management necessitates continuous monitoring of system performance and resource utilization. Tools such as 'top', 'htop', and 'glances' facilitate the real-time observation of processes, detailing their CPU and memory usage, as well as system load averages. Having access to this information empowers administrators to quickly identify rogue processes or those that may be consuming excessive resources. By integrating this monitoring with alerts for critical thresholds, administrators can proactively respond to potential issues before they manifest into significant problems.

One fundamental strategy for real-time process management is the adoption of dynamic resource allocation. Using Linux's built-in features, such as control groups (cgroups), administrators can restrict the amount of CPU and memory available to specific processes or groups of processes. This ensures that critical applications retain the necessary resources to function optimally while preventing less significant processes from consuming resources irresponsibly. These regulations can be adjusted on-the-fly, providing the flexibility needed to adapt to changing workloads.

In addition to allocation, adjusting priorities in real-time is a powerful aspect of process management. Utilizing the nice and renice commands allows administrators to dynamically alter the scheduling priority of processes. For example, if a particular process is found to be monopolizing CPU cycles, its priority can be reduced, allowing more critical processes to receive the CPU time they require. This method promotes a healthy distribution of resources over time while guaranteeing that high-priority tasks are executed promptly.

Furthermore, implementing automated scripts to manage real-time processes can enhance efficiency by reducing manual intervention. These scripts can monitor processes and make dynamic adjustments according to predefined rules or resource thresholds. For instance, a script might automatically lower the priority of processes that exceed specific CPU usage or terminate those that do not respond within a set period. Automation ensures that administrators can maintain oversight without being overwhelmed by the intricacies of managing multiple processes in real-time.

Another important aspect of real-time process management is optimizing inter-process communication (IPC) to facilitate efficient coordination among processes. Utilizing mechanisms such as message queues, shared memory, or pipes can enhance collaboration, allowing processes to exchange data rapidly without incurring substantial resource overhead. Streamlining IPC not only enhances overall system performance but also minimizes delays caused by slow data access or resource contention.

Moreover, adapting to specific use cases is essential. In environments where latency is critical—such as real-time applications or server infrastructures—real-time process management may involve implementing dedicated CPU scheduling policies that prioritize low-latency responses. The use of real-time scheduling classes ensures that processes requiring immediate attention receive the necessary CPU time without being delayed by other tasks.

As technology continues to advance, the future of real-time process management will be shaped by emerging trends in automation and artificial intelligence. Machine learning can contribute to the development of intelligent systems that predict process demands based on historical usage patterns and dynamically adjust resources accordingly. As systems learn from their experiences, administrators will need to embrace these innovations, integrating them into their methodologies for process management.

In conclusion, real-time process management is a crucial practice within Linux environments that ensures processes operate efficiently and maintain system responsiveness. By implementing dynamic resource allocation, adjusting process priorities, utilizing automation, optimizing IPC, and adapting to specific needs, administrators can effectively manage processes in real time. This proactive approach not only enhances performance but also cultivates a resilient and efficient system capable of meeting the demands of its users—much like an artist carefully tending to their creation, fostering balance and beauty. Embracing the principles of real-time process management empowers administrators to cultivate a seamless operational environment that thrives in responsiveness and efficiency.

12. Load Balancing for Optimal Performance

12.1. Concepts of Load Balancing

In the landscape of Linux system administration, the concept of load balancing emerges as a crucial technique to optimize resource management and maintain system performance. Load balancing can be compared to the intricate art of flower arrangement, where each element must be carefully positioned to achieve harmony and balance. This subchapter dives into the foundational concepts of load balancing, its significance in process management, and key strategies employed to ensure efficient distribution of workloads.

At its core, load balancing is the practice of distributing workloads evenly across multiple servers or resources to prevent any single point of overload. This process is vital in environments where multiple applications or services intersect, as uneven distribution can lead to bottlenecks, service degradation, or even downtime. By managing how resources are allocated among various processes, load balancing enables administrators to maximize system utilization while ensuring high availability and responsiveness.

One fundamental principle of load balancing is the concept of redundancy. By employing multiple servers to handle requests, even if one server fails or becomes overloaded, others can take over, maintaining service continuity. This redundancy not only enhances reliability but also facilitates fault tolerance, a critical aspect in mission-critical systems where uptime is paramount.

There are different methods and strategies for achieving load balancing, each tailored to specific use cases and requirements. The two primary types of load balancing are hardware-based and software-based solutions. Hardware load balancers are dedicated appliances designed to efficiently distribute traffic between servers, optimizing the connection process and improving resource utilization. Software-based load balancers, on the other hand, run on standard server hardware and can be configured for various applications, making them a versatile option for many environments.

Round-robin is one of the most common load balancing algorithms employed in both hardware and software solutions. In this technique, requests are directed to each server in a sequential manner, ensuring an even distribution of workloads. While simple and effective for evenly matched servers, round-robin may not account for differences in server capabilities or current loads.

Least connection load balancing is another popular strategy, which intelligently directs traffic to the server with the fewest active connections. This method is particularly effective in scenarios where server workloads may vary significantly. By monitoring and accommodating server capabilities, the least connection method helps ensure that each server maintains optimal levels of activity.

Another advanced technique is IP Hashing. In this method, a unique hash function is employed to determine the server assignment based on the client's IP address. This technique helps in maintaining session persistence, ensuring that users consistently connect to the same server throughout their interaction with an application.

Load balancing is also vital in cloud environments, where resource allocation can be very dynamic. Cloud-based load balancers can automatically scale resources up or down based on demand, assigning workloads efficiently to accommodate changing user loads. This adaptable approach significantly enhances resource utilization and minimizes costs associated with over-provisioning.

In addition to resource distribution, monitoring plays a critical role in effective load balancing. Administrators must incorporate monitoring tools that continuously assess server performance, analyze system metrics, and identify trends related to load patterns. Alerts can be automated to notify administrators of any anomalies or potential server overloads, allowing for swift intervention and adjustment to load balancing strategies.

Another key takeaway is the importance of regular testing. Administrators should periodically evaluate their load balancing configuration and effectiveness through simulated load tests, which can reveal areas for improvement or allow for the fine-tuning of algorithms and settings.

Finally, comprehensive documentation of load balancing configurations and their operational workflows can serve as a critical reference for system administrators. This documentation facilitates troubleshooting and enhances the understanding of dependencies among various components in the load balancing architecture, enabling quicker resolution of issues as they arise.

In conclusion, load balancing is an essential component of Linux process management that optimizes resource allocation and enhances system performance. By employing various strategies such as round-robin, least connections, and IP hashing, administrators can ensure efficient distribution of workloads and maintain system stability. The effective integration of monitoring practices, regular testing, and comprehensive documentation complements load balancing efforts, leading to robust and resilient environments where processes can thrive effectively. As administrators embrace these foundational principles of load balancing, they will cultivate an ecosystem capable of adapting to shifting demands while delivering high performance, similar to the artistry found in a finely crafted bouquet.

12.2. Tools and Strategies for Load Distribution

In the context of system administration within Linux environments, load distribution plays a crucial role in optimizing performance and ensuring system stability. Just as a skilled gardener balances the various elements of a landscape to support growth, effective load distribution balances server resources to meet user demands and operational needs. This section delves into the tools and strategies used to achieve efficient load distribution across processes, enhancing the overall responsiveness and reliability of Linux systems.

A foundational understanding of load distribution begins with the architecture of the system itself. In a typical multi-user environment, processes may comprise various applications, services, and background tasks, each with its own resource requirements. When processes compete for limited resources—CPU, memory, I/O, and network bandwidth—load distribution becomes essential. Distributing workloads prevents any single process from becoming a bottleneck, enabling the system to handle multiple tasks concurrently without performance degradation.

Among the primary tools for achieving effective load distribution is the use of load balancers, which distribute incoming network traffic across multiple servers or processes to ensure no single point of overload. By employing techniques such as round-robin routing, least-connections, or IP hashing, load balancers can provide an even and responsive experience for users. Load balancers can be hardware-based or software-based solutions such as Nginx or HAProxy, both of which are widely used to manage traffic efficiently.

In addition to load balancers, Linux systems can leverage kernel features such as cgroups (control groups). Cgroups allow administrators to allocate resources dynamically among processes based on their needs. By setting limits on CPU usage, memory, or I/O to specified process groups, administrators ensure that high-demand processes receive sufficient resources while limiting the impact of resource-heavy but less critical processes. This approach aids in maintaining overall system stability, as resource contention can lead to performance problems.

Moreover, process scheduling directly influences load distribution. The Completely Fair Scheduler (CFS) manages how processes are scheduled for execution on CPU cores, ensuring equitable distribution of CPU time among all runnable tasks. Utilizing scheduling algorithms effectively—such as setting process priorities or employing real-time scheduling classes where necessary—enables administrators to fine-tune how workloads are processed, impacting load distribution dynamically.

For environments that implement containerization, such as Docker, optimizing load distribution involves considering resource constraints and limits within each container. Administrators can utilize orchestration platforms like Kubernetes to automate resource allocation and scaling based on real-time demand, ensuring optimal load distribution across containerized applications. This dynamic adjustment allows organizations to respond quickly to changing workloads without manual intervention.

A significant aspect of effective load distribution is monitoring and analysis. Employing performance monitoring tools such as Prometheus, Grafana, or ELK Stack can provide detailed insights into how processes are consuming resources over time. By visualizing this data, administrators can identify trends and anomalies that indicate potential load distribution issues. Recognizing high-usage patterns allows for the proactive adjustment of process allocation, enhancing performance before degradation occurs.

In addition, administrators should adopt automated scaling solutions that respond to real-time load changes. Autoscaling mechanisms can be implemented in cloud environments to dynamically adjust resources based on predefined rules. For example, once CPU utilization exceeds a certain threshold, the system can automatically provision additional server instances or distribute the load more evenly across existing processes, reducing the risk of performance bottlenecks.

Understanding the dependencies between processes is essential as well. Administrators need to ensure that dependent processes receive adequate resources while also managing the loads of upstream and downstream tasks. Tools like htop and ps can assist in visualizing these relationships, allowing for smarter decisions regarding resource allocations and process adjustments.

Finally, communication within teams remains pivotal. Engaging with users, developers, and stakeholders to understand their resource needs and performance expectations aids in designing a load distribution strategy that fits the unique context of the organization. This collaborative approach fosters a culture of proactive process management, where all users feel empowered to contribute.

In summary, the tools and strategies for load distribution in Linux systems focus on balancing resources effectively to optimize performance and stability. By employing load balancers, utilizing cgroups, demonstrating effective scheduling practices, monitoring resource usage, and embracing automation, administrators can cultivate a system that efficiently meets the demands of users and processes alike. Ultimately, mastering these components transforms process management into an art form, ensuring that Linux systems flourish and thrive under varying loads and demands, akin to a well-managed garden of diverse plants harmoniously coexisting and thriving together.

12.3. Adaptive Load Balancing Techniques

In the context of effective system administration, adaptive load balancing techniques have emerged as essential strategies for optimizing resource distribution and maintaining operational efficiency in Linux environments. Just as a garden requires careful attention to the distribution of water and nutrients among plants, effective load management ensures that processes receive the appropriate resources to thrive without overrunning the system's capabilities. This section delves into various adaptive load balancing techniques that administrators can implement to ensure smooth, responsive system performance.

Adaptive load balancing involves continuously assessing real-time performance metrics to dynamically distribute workload across available resources. The essence of adaptability lies in its ability to respond not only to current demands but also to changing conditions, making it vital in environments where workloads can fluctuate dramatically. By employing a combination of strategies and tools, system administrators can enhance their adaptive load balancing capabilities.

One of the most critical techniques is the use of intelligent algorithms that can dynamically adjust the distribution of resources based on real-time analysis. Load balancing algorithms, such as weighted round-robin or least-connections, allow administrators to allocate work to servers or processes that are best equipped to handle the load at that moment. Implementing these strategies in conjunction with monitoring tools ensures that workloads are distributed evenly, minimizing contention and latency while maximizing throughput.

Moreover, leveraging container orchestration solutions like Kubernetes further enhances adaptive load balancing. Kubernetes automatically adjusts the distribution of processes based on resource demands, scaling instances of services up or down as needed. This dynamic capability enables organizations to respond quickly to peaks in demand without overcommitting resources, providing a comprehensive solution to managing workloads effectively.

In addition to algorithms and orchestration, utilizing caching mechanisms is a vital technique for adaptive load balancing. By caching frequently accessed data, systems can offload requests from databases or backend services, leading to improved response times. Adaptive caching involves monitoring access patterns and dynamically adjusting cache levels based on current resource availability and server load. When integrated with load balancing strategies, caching helps streamline processes, resulting in a more responsive user experience.

Another adaptive load balancing technique leverages real-time analytics and predictive algorithms to foresee fluctuations in demand. By analyzing historical data trends and modeling potential future loads, administrators can proactively adjust resource allocations before bottlenecks occur. This foresight allows organizations to preemptively scale their infrastructure, ensuring that adequate resources are available during times of peak demand.

Moreover, balancing client-server workloads is crucial in maintaining optimal performance. This balance involves assessing the resource requirements of both client and server processes to ensure they operate effectively in unison. Custom routing strategies can be employed to direct client requests to servers best suited for the task, bolstering efficiency and response times.

Implementing health checks is an essential aspect of adaptive load balancing. By continuously monitoring the health of processes and servers, the system can automatically reroute traffic from failing or overloaded resources to healthy ones. This measure enhances reliability and ensures that end-users consistently receive optimal performance.

As organizations increasingly adopt microservices architectures, incorporating adaptive load balancing within this context requires unique considerations. Each microservice can be independently scaled and managed, allowing for flexible load distribution across our services. Understanding how these services interact, defining service dependencies, and monitoring their performance are essential for maintaining an adaptive approach.

Finally, documentation and collaboration remain critical. Ensuring that adaptive load balancing strategies are well-documented allows teams to replicate successful approaches and modify techniques as circumstances evolve. The ongoing communication between system administrators, developers, and users fosters a collaborative environment where specific performance requirements can be accurately captured and addressed.

In conclusion, adaptive load balancing techniques are indispensable for managing resource distribution in Linux environments. By leveraging intelligent algorithms, orchestration tools, caching mechanisms, predictive analytics, and robust monitoring, administrators can optimize system performance while maintaining responsiveness to user demands. This holistic approach, characterized by adaptability and proactive management, ultimately fosters an environment where processes excel and resources are utilized efficiently, akin to a flourishing garden nurtured through careful planning and cultivation. The ongoing pursuit of refining adaptive load balancing techniques will continue to be a focal point for Linux system administrators in the quest to enhance performance and resilience in an ever-evolving technological landscape.

12.4. Balancing Between Servers and Clients

Balancing the demands between servers and clients is fundamental to achieving a well-functioning, responsive Linux environment. The dynamic interplay between client requests and server processing capabilities sets the stage for successful interactions, maintenance of performance benchmarks, and ultimately the satisfaction of users and applications alike. This balance is particularly crucial in contemporary IT infrastructures where systems are under constant pressure from variable workloads and client expectations.

In a typical scenario, servers host services or applications that respond to requests from clients. The server must efficiently allocate its resources—CPU, memory, and I/O—to process these requests without becoming overloaded. Conversely, clients must optimally utilize the services available to them, ensuring their requests are fulfilled swiftly and accurately. Striking the right balance is key to managing this relationship effectively.

One of the first steps in achieving this balance is accurately assessing resource usage on both the server side and the client side. On the server side, tools such as 'top', 'htop', 'vmstat', and 'iostat' provide real-time metrics that help administrators identify how much CPU and memory each service or application is consuming. Having visuals of server load averaged over 1, 5, and 15 minutes can inform decisions about whether to scale resources up or down based on current demands. If a service consistently operates at peak capacity, it may be time to increase the allocated resources or optimize the application code.

On the client side, understanding user behavior and the nature of client requests is equally important. Monitoring tools can capture which requests are commonly made, their frequency, and the response times from the server. By identifying patterns in client usage, administrators can optimize server configurations (e.g., caching frequent requests) to enhance performance and reduce latency for end-users. This requires fluid communication between application developers and system administrators to ensure that server capacity and client expectations align efficiently.

Another critical factor for balancing server-client demands is understanding the impact of network conditions, as networking plays a significant role in the speed and efficiency of client-server interactions. Server tuning for network performance, alongside client optimizations—such as using content delivery networks (CDNs) or employing caching strategies—can drastically improve the responsiveness of applications. Tools such as `iftop` or `netstat` can help assess the bandwidth usage and performance of network interfaces, guiding decisions to optimize communication pathways.

Furthermore, implementing quality of service (QoS) policies can help prioritize traffic according to specific requirements. By ensuring that critical applications receive bandwidth over less critical traffic, administrators can optimize the balance further for both clients and servers. This requires a holistic view of system demands and an understanding of how different processes interact with network resources.

Automation plays a vital role in maintaining the balance between servers and clients. By utilizing orchestration and automation tools (like Kubernetes) along with monitoring systems, administrators can dynamically allocate resources based on real-time traffic patterns. For instance, if traffic spikes for a particular application, Kubernetes could spin up additional instances to handle the load, ensuring that clients receive timely responses.

Lastly, regular assessments and feedback loops become essential for fine-tuning this balance over time. Creating frameworks for logging and monitoring both server and client performance can yield valuable data that informs subsequent decisions regarding resource allocation, process management, and system configuration. Building a culture of continuous improvement involving users, developers, and operational teams contributes to an evolving understanding of needs, enhancing both server responsiveness and client interactions.

In summary, balancing the demands between servers and clients involves utilizing monitoring tools, assessing resource usage, optimizing network performance, implementing automation, and establishing regular feedback loops. By marrying technology with an adaptive strategy, IT administrators can create an environment where servers efficiently serve clients while maintaining peak performance and responsiveness. This harmony mirrors the careful equilibrium sought in artforms such as bonsai cultivation, where attentiveness to details leads to a flourishing outcome—one that benefits both the service provider and the end users they support.

12.5. Monitoring and Adjusting Balancing Efforts

In the larger context of managing a Linux system efficiently, monitoring and adjusting balancing efforts among processes is paramount. As the system operates, it is fundamental to continuously assess the health of workloads, ensuring they are properly distributed and aligned with available resources. This dynamic management approach not only enhances performance but also stabilizes the environment against potential threats of overload or system failure.

Successfully balancing system loads involves utilizing various tools and techniques that enable administrators to monitor active processes in real-time. Tools such as 'top' or 'htop' provide memorable snapshots of running processes, showing administrators exactly where resources are allocated and if bottlenecks emerge. High CPU or memory usage by a particular process may signal an imbalance that requires immediate attention. For instance, an administrator may note that a high-load application is consistently consuming more CPU cycles than expected, thus influencing overall system responsiveness. This awareness enables informed decisions regarding resource adjustments.

Once an issue is identified, corrective action can be tailored accordingly. Adjustments may involve redistributing resources through the renice command, which alters the scheduling priority of a process to ensure that more urgent tasks receive the necessary CPU time. For example, lowering the priority of background tasks can alleviate strain on critical services experiencing heavy load, ensuring that user-facing applications remain operational and responsive.

Moreover, establishing automated monitoring and alert systems enhances the effectiveness of balancing efforts. By utilizing tools like Nagios, administrators can set thresholds to trigger alerts when resource usage exceeds defined limits. This allows for swift actions in rebalancing workloads before performance dips significantly impact users. Automation scripts can also be employed to respond dynamically to these alerts, facilitating process adjustments or reconfigurations without requiring manual intervention.

Furthermore, while responding to imbalances in real-time is essential, proactive planning forms the backbone of effective resource management. By maintaining detailed logs and conducting regular inspections of process behaviors, administrators can create predictive models of resource allocations, informing future workload distributions. Tools such as Grafana and Prometheus offer visualization and analysis capabilities that unveil usage trends over time, enabling more strategic planning for resource allocation in anticipation of changing demands.

Documentation also plays a crucial role in monitoring and adjusting balancing efforts. Keeping detailed records of processes, their load patterns, and the actions taken in response to specific situations establishes a knowledge base that can aid future decision-making. This documentation can inform processes for others and provide critical context for troubleshooting should problems arise.

Additionally, load testing becomes imperative when considering system changes that could drastically impact resource distributions. By simulating different workloads, administrators assess how current configurations hold up under strain, allowing them to develop strategies for load balancing based on empirical performance data rather than instinct.

Ultimately, promoting communication among team members around processes, resource usage, and issues encountered is necessary for a cohesive process management strategy. Involving application developers and end-users in discussions regarding resource requirements fosters a collaborative culture, ensuring that system performance aligns with real-world needs.

In conclusion, monitoring and adjusting balancing efforts among processes is a continuous, proactive activity crucial to maintaining an efficient Linux system. By utilizing the right tools for real-time monitoring, establishing automated responses, conducting careful documentation, and promoting open communication, system administrators can successfully navigate the complexities of workload management. This intricate balancing act ultimately contributes to a responsive, reliable, and high-performing Linux environment, ensuring that both users and applications receive the resources needed to thrive.

13. Protecting System Integrity Through Process Management

13.1. Recognizing Malicious Processes

In the realm of system administration, recognizing malicious processes is a essential skill that underscores the importance of vigilance and proactive monitoring in maintaining the integrity and security of a Linux environment. Just as a gardener must be keenly aware of the signs of pests that threaten a flourishing garden, system administrators must be adept at identifying abnormal behavior within processes that may signal potential security threats or system malfunctions.

Malicious processes can manifest in various forms, whether as malware designed to exploit vulnerabilities, unauthorized applications running under a user's context, or legitimate applications that have been compromised. The goal for system administrators is to establish a robust framework for detecting and responding to such threats before they can escalate into significant issues.

The first step in recognizing malicious processes involves establishing a baseline of normal system behavior. This can be achieved by continuously monitoring processes and their resource usage patterns. Using tools such as 'top', 'htop', or 'ps', administrators can record typical CPU and memory usage ranges for applications over time. Any deviation from these patterns—such as sudden spikes in CPU usage by a previously benign process—may warrant further investigation as it could indicate a malicious activity.

Another effective approach is leveraging process integrity monitoring tools that watch for unauthorized changes to processes. For example, tools like Tripwire or OSSEC can be configured to monitor for changes in process states or configurations, alerting administrators if processes deviate from expected behaviors or if new, unrecognized processes start running. These system integrity tools often include a baseline snapshot of legitimate processes, making it easier to spot anomalies.

It is also advisable to take advantage of advanced threat detection solutions. Technologies such as intrusion detection systems (IDS) can monitor system logs for suspicious activity related to processes, helping identify potential threats in real-time. These systems analyze patterns of behavior rather than simply known signatures, allowing them to catch zero-day exploits that might bypass traditional antivirus solutions.

Another crucial technique is scrutinizing process parent-child relationships. Malicious processes are often spawned by legitimate applications to obscure their presence. By using commands like pstree, administrators can visualize the hierarchy of running processes and pinpoint suspicious tree structures—such as processes that appear anomalous given their parents. A web server spawning unfamiliar network processes, for instance, should raise flags for further inspection.

Network activity also serves as an invaluable indicator of malicious processes. Monitoring tools like iftop and tcpdump can be used to detect abnormal network traffic patterns from individual processes. Processes attempting communication on unusual ports or utilizing atypical protocols may suggest nefarious activity. Establishing alerts for unusual outbound connections can provide valuable insights into possible data exfiltration or command-and-control communications by compromised processes.

Conducting regular audits of active processes against known malicious software databases can provide another layer of protection. Tools such as chkrootkit and rkhunter serve to scan Linux systems for rootkits and other forms of malware. Regularly scheduling these scans can detect instances of malicious processes early, allowing administrators to take swift action.

Once malicious processes are identified, prompt action must be taken to contain the threat. This could include isolating the affected system from the network, terminating the malicious processes, and conducting a thorough investigation to determine the vector of compromise.

Following containment, a careful strategy should be devised to remediate vulnerabilities that allowed the threat to materialize. This may involve applying software updates, altering user permissions, or enhancing firewall rules.

Lastly, fostering a culture of cybersecurity awareness is vital within any organization. Conducting regular training sessions for users about recognizing suspicious processes and potential social engineering tactics will cultivate a more vigilant user base. Empowering users can enhance the overall security posture of the system, assisting administrators in their efforts to maintain healthy processes.

In conclusion, recognizing malicious processes is an ongoing effort that requires a combination of establishing baselines, monitoring systems, analyzing network activity, and employing appropriate detection tools. By adopting comprehensive strategies for process oversight, Linux administrators can proactively safeguard their systems, ensuring that operational integrity remains intact amidst the evolving threat landscape. Ultimately, an elevated awareness of potential malicious activity mirrors the attentive care of a gardener, nurturing a secure environment where processes can flourish in safety.

13.2. Implementing Process Isolation

Implementing process isolation is a key strategy in modern Linux system management, designed to enhance security and stability within computing environments. This approach focuses on preventing processes from interfering with one another, thereby safeguarding system integrity and isolating potentially harmful actions. Understanding and effectively applying process isolation techniques is essential for any administrator looking to maintain a robust and resilient Linux environment.

At its core, process isolation ensures that each process runs in its own protected environment, thereby minimizing the risk of data corruption, security breaches, or system crashes. This concept can be compared to setting up separate areas in a garden to cultivate different types of plants; by isolating them, you prevent diseases or pests from spreading, allowing each plant to flourish independently.

One of the most effective methods for implementing process isolation in Linux is through the use of namespaces. Namespaces create virtualized environments that encapsulate certain aspects of a process's execution context—such as process IDs, mount points, network interfaces, and user IDs—ensuring that a process can only see its own resources and has limited visibility of others. For example, the implementation of User Namespaces allows applications to run with reduced privileges while maintaining access to necessary resources, effectively closing gaps that could be exploited by a potential attacker.

Another powerful mechanism is the use of cgroups (control groups), which allows administrators to allocate and limit system resources to specific processes or groups of processes. By managing CPU and memory usage through cgroups, administrators can isolate processes from one another and control the total resources they consume. This form of resource allocation is vital in preventing a single process from overwhelming the system and affecting the performance of other processes.

Additionally, employing containerization technologies like Docker or Kubernetes allows for robust process isolation. Containers inherently embrace the isolation strategies discussed, encapsulating apps in self-contained environments that use the underlying kernel but operate independently of one another. In this way, applications can run without fear of affecting each other, all while being lightweight and resource-efficient. Through orchestrating these containers, administrators can deploy, manage, and operate applications without worrying about dependencies or process conflicts.

The implementation of seccomp (secure computing mode) further enhances process isolation by allowing administrators to restrict the system calls a process can make. This creates a safeguard against malicious exploitation, as it limits the operational capabilities of applications to only those necessary for their successful execution. By reducing the attack surface of processes through stringent seccomp policies, administrators can protect against many common vulnerabilities.

To complement these strategies, it's vital to incorporate strong access control mechanisms. Utilizing tools like SELinux (Security-Enhanced Linux) or AppArmor provides an additional layer of security, allowing policies to define what resources processes can access and how they can interact with one another. By enabling mandatory access control, administrators can create strict boundaries around processes, mitigating the risk of privilege escalation or unauthorized access.

Monitoring for deviations in typical process behavior is also crucial in upholding process isolation. Employing tools like auditd allows administrators to keep logs of access and execution events by processes. By analyzing these logs, they can identify anomalies that may indicate a process is attempting to breach its designated isolation boundary.

Finally, maintaining clear documentation of isolated environments, roles, and responsibilities in the process landscape becomes essential over time. As systems evolve, understanding the context and configurations of isolated processes helps administrators respond to incidents and adapt to changes without compromising security or efficiency.

In conclusion, implementing process isolation in Linux environments is fundamental for ensuring system integrity and security. By utilizing namespaces, cgroups, containerization technologies, seccomp, and access controls like SELinux, administrators can create robust barriers between processes. Continuous monitoring and documentation further enrich these efforts, ultimately fostering a resilient and secure operating environment. As administrators embrace process isolation techniques, they effectively cultivate a Linux system akin to a vibrant garden, where each plant thrives in its designated space, contributing to the ecosystem's overall vitality and integrity.

13.3. Controlling and Limiting Process Capabilities

Controlling and limiting process capabilities is an essential practice in the realm of Linux system administration. By understanding and implementing these controls, administrators can enhance the security of their operating environments and maintain optimal system performance. This subchapter explores the various techniques, tools, and best practices to effectively manage process capabilities, thereby safeguarding against potential threats and ensuring resource efficiency.

At the outset, it is crucial to recognize that Linux processes operate with specific capabilities that allow them to interact with the system's resources. These capabilities are a set of privileges that define what actions processes can perform, such as accessing files, managing networks, or modifying system configurations. By default, processes inherit the capabilities of the user running them, which may grant them more access than necessary. This can pose security risks, as a compromised process could exploit its capabilities to perform malicious actions.

To mitigate such risks, administrators can employ the principle of least privilege when assigning process capabilities. This principle dictates that processes should only have the minimum necessary privileges to perform their required tasks. By limiting capabilities, administrators reduce the attack surface, making it more difficult for malicious actors to exploit vulnerabilities within the system.

One effective way to control process capabilities is by utilizing Linux's capabilities framework. This allows administrators to fine-tune the access permissions assigned to processes, ensuring they can only perform specific actions relevant to their intended operations. Tools such as setcap and getcap can be employed to set and view capabilities on executables, allowing for precise control over what each process can do. For example:

```
setcap cap_net_bind_service=+ep my_service
```

This command grants the my_service executable the ability to bind to network ports below 1024 without needing to run as the root user, exemplifying how capabilities can be tailored to enhance security while maintaining functionality.

Another key strategy for controlling process capabilities involves using chroot jails or containers. By placing processes within a chroot environment, administrators can isolate them from the rest of the system, effectively limiting their access to the filesystem and other processes. This added layer of security ensures that even if a process is compromised, its impact on the overall system is contained. Containerization technologies like Docker or Kubernetes offer similar isolation, encapsulating applications with their dependencies in self-sufficient environments.

Security modules like SELinux (Security-Enhanced Linux) and AppArmor also play a pivotal role in controlling and limiting process capabilities. These security frameworks allow administrators to define policies that restrict what processes can do based on their contexts. By enforcing granular security controls, SELinux and AppArmor ensure that even processes with elevated privileges cannot perform actions that violate established security policies. Regularly reviewing and updating these policies is integral to maintaining a robust security posture.

Monitoring tools are essential for overseeing processes and their capabilities. Tools like ps, htop, and specialized security auditing tools can be employed to check for unauthorized or suspicious processes running on the system. These tools can help identify processes that have acquired excessive privileges or behave anomalously. Implementing automated scripts or alerting systems can further enhance monitoring, allowing administrators to be quickly notified of any potential threats.

Additionally, logging process actions and auditing capabilities forms a crucial part of controlling process behaviors. Keeping detailed logs of process executions, their associated capabilities, and any changes made through tools like auditd can aid in identifying security breaches or misconfigurations. Periodically reviewing these logs allows administrators to detect trends or anomalies that may indicate potential vulnerabilities.

Lastly, training system users and developers about secure coding practices can also positively impact process capability management. By encouraging development teams to design applications that adhere to the principle of least privilege, administrators can minimize the risk of vulnerabilities being introduced through process mismanagement.

In conclusion, controlling and limiting process capabilities are vital components of effective Linux system administration. By employing the principles of least privilege, utilizing the capabilities framework, isolating processes, enforcing security policies, monitoring active processes, and implementing logging strategies, administrators can enhance security and optimize resource management. This careful orchestration of process controls is essential for fostering a resilient and secure operating environment, allowing the Linux system to operate efficiently and defend against potential threats, much like tending to a delicate bonsai to ensure its continued vitality and growth.

13.4. Auditing Process Actions

In the realm of process management, ensuring a seamless flow of activities relies heavily on a thorough understanding of the auditing process actions.

Auditing process actions in a Linux environment forms the backbone of effective system administration, aiding in monitoring, compliance, security, and troubleshooting activities. It involves the systematic recording of all operations performed by processes, capturing key information such as user interactions, resource allocations, and status changes. By establishing robust auditing practices, administrators can maintain elevated transparency and oversight, detect anomalies, and ensure that necessary actions are taken to preserve system integrity.

The process of auditing entails tracking a multitude of activities that processes perform. Each entry typically includes a timestamp, the user who initiated the action, the process ID (PID), the executable name, the resources involved, and any significant events (such as errors or privilege changes). This information becomes invaluable when diagnosing system performance issues or breaches.

A fundamental tool in this process is the Linux Audit framework, which provides a mechanism for auditing system calls, file accesses, and process activities. By configuring the audit system with the `auditd` daemon, administrators can specify which events to track. For instance, one might audit all commands executed by users or monitor specific system files that are critical to security. Regularly examining the generated audit logs allows administrators to quickly assess actions taken by any process and identify unintended changes or malicious activities.

Moreover, it is advisable to establish clear policies around what needs to be audited based on organizational needs. For example, in environments handling sensitive data, comprehensive auditing of all processes that access that data is paramount. Administrators can use tools like `ausearch` to retrieve and analyze audit records based on specific criteria, allowing for streamlined investigations.

In addition to continuous monitoring, implementing proactive response mechanisms is vital in the auditing process. These mechanisms can include automated alerts triggered by specified criteria —such as a process attempting to access sensitive areas of the file system or unexpectedly exiting. This approach not only enhances the response to potential threats but also fosters a culture of monitoring and accountability among users.

Furthermore, establishing a retention policy for audit logs is critical. Regular archiving and secure storage of these logs not only assist in compliance with regulatory requirements but also provide a historical record essential for forensic analysis in the event of a security breach. Administrators should regularly evaluate storage capacity for logs and overwrite policies to mitigate risks of data loss.

Another aspect to consider is integrating audit logging with other security tools. For example, combining audit logs with intrusion detection systems (IDS) can enrich the security landscape of the environment. This integration can trigger alerts based on suspicious activities, providing layered security protection through cross-reference checks.

Finally, conducting regular reviews of the audit logs and processes highlighted in them will help ensure that actions are taken based on the insights gleaned. These reviews lead to better process optimization and security practices, informing administrators about common user behaviors, unexpected process activities, and potential misconduct.

In conclusion, auditing process actions is integral to maintaining a secure, efficient, and compliant Linux environment. By implementing systematic logging, establishing clear policies, responding to anomalies, securing archived logs, integrating tools, and reviewing findings, administrators can cultivate a culture of accountability and reliability. Just as a gardener might meticulously record the growth of each plant to ensure a lush environment, so too must system administrators monitor the actions of processes to guarantee the ongoing health and resilience of their Linux systems. Through diligent auditing practices, they enhance operational integrity and responsiveness, paving the way for a secure and efficient computing ecosystem.

13.5. Designing a Secure Process Framework

Designing a secure process framework is vital for any Linux system administrator tasked with ensuring both the efficiency and security of processes within their systems. A well-structured process framework not only facilitates seamless operation and interaction between various components and applications but also protects sensitive data and resources from unauthorized access or malicious activities.

To begin, the foundation of a secure process framework lies in understanding the concepts of least privilege and isolation. The principle of least privilege posits that users and processes should only have the minimal level of access required to perform their tasks. This principle applies to process creation where developers should strive to limit capabilities associated with processes. For instance, processes that handle sensitive information should operate under restricted permissions that prevent them from executing arbitrary commands or accessing unrelated system files.

The isolation of processes is achieved using various techniques and tools that encapsulate processes and manage their interactions. Namespaces and control groups (cgroups) are essential in this regard. Namespaces provide a way to create isolated environments for processes, allowing them to operate independently while still interacting with shared system resources. Cgroups, on the other hand, allow administrators to allocate and enforce resource limits on processes, ensuring that no single process can monopolize CPU or memory usage. Together, these tools create an environment where processes can thrive without the risk of interference.

Process capabilities also play a crucial role in the design of a secure framework. Such capabilities govern what specific actions a process can perform based on its context, enabling administrators to grant only the necessary privileges. By using tools like setcap, administrators can configure capabilities for executables while adhering to the least privilege principle. For instance, allowing a web server process to bind to privileged ports without granting it full root access preserves a balance between functionality and security.

Additionally, incorporating effective logging mechanisms into your process framework provides critical insights into process actions and potential security threats. By auditing process activity through logging and monitoring tools, administrators can track actions performed by processes, identify anomalies, and respond quickly to unreliable or suspicious behaviors. Tools like auditd can centralize evaluation, capturing successful and unsuccessful process-related actions for further analysis, helping to reinforce security.

Equally important is the concept of continuous monitoring to maintain process integrity. System monitoring tools that integrate with the process framework can alert administrators of unusual process behaviors, including excessive CPU or memory usage, unexpected changes in process state, or unauthorized access attempts. These alerts empower administrators to react swiftly and mitigate potential threats before they escalate into security breaches.

Establishing a backup and recovery plan for critical process information fortifies the security framework. Configuring regular backups allows for quick restoration in the event of a breach or failure. Additionally, version control systems can be utilized to manage configurations associated with processes, facilitating seamless rollbacks when necessary.

Furthermore, enhancing process security through regular updates and patch management is paramount for protecting against vulnerabilities. Keeping the operating system and applications updated mitigates the risk of exploiting known weaknesses and ensures adherence to the latest security practices.

Training and education are also essential components of a secure process design framework. Encouraging developers and system users alike to engage in secure coding practices helps prevent the introduction of vulnerabilities during the application development lifecycle. Workshops and seminars provide insights into threats and best practices, fostering a culture of security awareness.

Lastly, conducting regular security audits is crucial in evaluating the effectiveness of your secure process framework. By reviewing processes, dependencies, and access policies, administrators can identify areas for improvement and address vulnerabilities before they can be exploited.

In conclusion, designing a secure process framework in Linux encompasses the principles of least privilege, process isolation, effective logging, continuous monitoring, proactive security measures, and ongoing education and auditing. By implementing these components, system administrators can protect their environments from malicious activities while optimizing resource allocation and process efficiency. An effective secure process framework ultimately fosters a robust operational environment poised to respond to the demands of users and applications alike, akin to nurturing a flourishing bonsai tree through a careful balance of growth and restraint.

14. System Failures and Recovery Management

14.1. Understanding System Crash Dynamics

In the landscape of Linux system administration, understanding system crash dynamics is vital for effective recovery and resilience. System crashes can arise from a multitude of causes, ranging from hardware failures and kernel panics to application errors and resource exhaustion. Each of these incidents can have significant consequences, including data loss, downtime, and diminished performance. By analyzing the causes and effects of system crashes, administrators can develop robust strategies that facilitate swift recovery and minimize disruptions.

The causes of system crashes often originate from deeper underlying issues. Hardware failures, such as malfunctioning disks, RAM errors, or overheating components, can lead to abrupt system shutdowns. In such scenarios, identifying failing hardware through monitoring tools and performing regular diagnostic checks can be proactive measures to mitigate the risk of crashes. On the software side, kernel panics can occur due to bugs within the kernel or drivers, leading to a complete halt of the operating system. Understanding these vulnerabilities, and having a robust testing and patching strategy, can limit the potential for such incidents.

Application errors also pose a significant risk for system stability. Bugs, memory leaks, or poor programming practices can lead to processes consuming excessive resources, resulting in system-wide slowdowns or crashes. Operating under the principle of least privilege, where applications are given only the necessary permissions, can help limit the impact of application-level failures. Additionally, the careful design of applications—including reasonable error handling and resource management practices—can contribute effectively to preventing crashes.

Resource exhaustion is another common cause of system instability. When a system runs out of critical resources—such as CPU cycles, memory, or disk space—processes may fail, leading to cascading effects on overall system stability. Implementing resource quotas to limit how much a single process can consume, together with effective monitoring strategies, can maintain the balance of resources. Ensuring that alerts are triggered when system thresholds are approached also provides an avenue for proactive management.

When a crash occurs, understanding the consequences is equally important. System downtime can adversely impact productivity, leading to disrupted services for users or customers. Data loss is another significant risk, particularly if processes are not adequately managed or if critical files are not backed up before the failure. Incorporating robust backup solutions and establishing disaster recovery plans can greatly mitigate these issues, ensuring that data is recoverable without excessive downtime.

To facilitate effective recovery following a crash, systematic strategies need to be implemented. One such strategy involves utilizing logging and monitoring systems to capture detailed information about system activity prior to the crash. Tools like `syslog`, `journalctl`, and application logs are instrumental for diagnosing the events leading up to a failure. This historical data enables administrators to trace back the steps that resulted in a crash, allowing for targeted fixes.

Another key element of recovery management involves leveraging tools designed for automatic recovery after crashes. For example, certain applications have built-in mechanisms to restart themselves after crashes, while supervisors like `systemd`, `supervisord`, or `monit` can manage process health and restart them when necessary. Creating resiliency through auto-recovery mechanisms ensures that business operations can continue with minimal interruption.

Educating staff on how to respond to system failures is essential for managing crash dynamics. Building a culture where processes and protocols are regularly reviewed enhances overall response effectiveness. This preparedness allows for an organized approach during crisis situations, improving recovery times.

In conclusion, understanding system crash dynamics encompasses a thorough analysis of causes and consequences, alongside implementing robust strategies for recovery. By identifying potential risks, analyzing crash incidents, utilizing logging and monitoring tools, and educating staff, administrators can develop a resilient Linux environment capable of swift recovery following failures. Such practices ensure that the operational integrity of systems is maintained, allowing organizations to flourish even amidst challenges, much like a well-tended bonsai that withstands adversities through careful oversight and nurturing. As technology continues to evolve, maintaining this awareness and adaptability will prove crucial in enhancing overall system resilience and performance.

14.2. Strategies for Process-Level Recovery

In the modern landscape of Linux system administration, effectively recovering from process-level faults is paramount for maintaining operational continuity and performance. The intricate interplay of processes within a Linux system can create vulnerabilities; thus, having robust recovery strategies in place is essential. This section will outline comprehensive procedures for recovering from such faults, focusing on proactive approaches, diagnostic techniques, and defined protocols for process management.

The fundamental step in developing a recovery strategy begins with comprehensive monitoring of process health and performance. Administrators should implement real-time monitoring systems that provide insights into running processes, allowing them to detect abnormalities or failures before they escalate. Tools such as 'top', 'htop', and 'ps' enable visibility into resource consumption patterns and process statuses, highlighting any instances of failure or excessive resource usage.

Once a fault is detected, promptly assessing the problem is crucial. Administrators must analyze logs using commands like journalctl, dmesg, and application-specific log files to determine the cause behind the failure. Understanding whether the fault stemmed from resource exhaustion, excessive load, a bug in the application, or malicious activity will dictate the approach for recovery.

When dealing with a crashed process, the first step is typically to restart the affected service. This can be done using service management commands like `systemctl restart <service>` for systemd managed services. It is critical to ensure that the underlying issue causing the crash is addressed before the process is restarted to avoid repeated failures.

If a process fails frequently, deeper investigation into its dependencies may be necessary. Identifying whether the failure relates to resource contention, library incompatibilities, or other dependent processes allows for targeted remediation. In cases where ongoing instability is evident, allocating more resources to the impacted process or adjusting its priority with `renice` can alleviate the load.

For processes that are critical and cannot afford extended downtime, implementing an automatic recovery mechanism becomes beneficial. Supervisors such as `systemd`, `supervisord`, or `monit` can monitor processes and restart them automatically upon a fault. This feature greatly reduces the need for manual intervention, allowing for quicker recovery times and minimized service disruption.

Incorporating version control into processes can help in recovering from faults systematically. Maintaining a versioning system for scripts and configurations allows administrators to revert to a stable state should a process fail due to recent changes. This disaster recovery strategy is essential for environments where rapid recovery operations are necessary.

Furthermore, if the process failure stems from configuration issues, revisiting deployment practices becomes essential. Scrutinizing deployment scripts and performance configurations ensures that processes operate under the best conditions possible. For persistent faults, running brief tests in a staging environment can aid in preemptively mitigating issues that might arise during production.

The role of automated testing cannot be overstated when it comes to recovering from faults. Employing continuous integration and deployment (CI/CD) methodologies allows for rigorous testing, ensuring that any changes made to processes are validated prior to deployment. Including robust test cases can reveal potential issues early, safeguarding against faults that might otherwise compromise processes.

Documentation is another vital component in recovery management. Creating a playbook that outlines recovery procedures, troubleshooting steps, and contact points for critical services helps streamline the response to process failures. This ensures continuity of operations across team members who may respond to an incident, providing clarity and minimizing confusion during crises.

Lastly, conducting a post-mortem analysis after a significant process fault is critical for learning and improvement. By evaluating what went wrong, how the recovery was handled, and identifying areas for process optimization, administrators can bolster their systems against future failures. This reflective exercise aids in refining processes, implementations, and responses to ensure a more resilient infrastructure.

In essence, recovering from process-level faults is not merely a reactive operation; it requires proactive monitoring, rapid assessment, and systematic intervention strategies. Integrating tools that facilitate automatic restarts, utilizing logging practices for diagnostic clarity, employing robust testing frameworks, and fostering a culture of documentation and reflection enhances an administrator's ability to manage processes effectively. By establishing these comprehensive procedures and maintaining a keen awareness of processes, system administrators can ensure operational continuity and optimize performance in their Linux environments.

14.3. Automatic Recovery Tools

Automatic Recovery Tools play an essential role in enhancing the resilience and stability of Linux environments by providing mechanisms to swiftly restore processes and services following a failure. In dynamic computing landscapes, where uptime and reliability are paramount, implementing tools and strategies that automate recovery procedures becomes indispensable. This section explores a variety of automatic recovery solutions, their functionalities, and how they can be effectively integrated to maintain operational continuity.

At the core of automatic recovery tools is the concept of process supervision, wherein specific services or processes are continuously monitored. Should a monitored process fail or become unresponsive, the tooling facilitates its automatic restart. Systemd, the default init system for many Linux distributions, embodies this functionality through its built-in service management capabilities. By configuring a service file with directives such as `Restart=always` or `Restart=on-failure`, administrators can ensure that critical services automatically restart upon failure, minimizing downtime.

Alongside systemd, tools like `supervisord` and `monit` provide versatile options for process management and monitoring in server environments. Supervisord, for example, enables the management of multiple processes while applying defined rules for automatic restarts, additional logging, and monitoring capabilities. This versatility can be particularly useful for applications requiring robust oversight and accountability, offering an intuitive interface for managing process states.

For environments relying heavily on containerization, orchestration solutions like Kubernetes also offer recovery functionalities. Kubernetes employs a declarative model where administrators define desired states for applications. If a pod (the smallest deployable unit in Kubernetes) becomes unavailable, the system automatically replaces it, ensuring that the desired number of replicas runs seamlessly. The inherent self-healing capabilities of Kubernetes enhance the reliability of applications running in containers and significantly reduce the operational burden on administrators.

On the monitoring front, integrating automatic recovery tools with logging and alerting systems promotes better visibility into process health. Automation platforms can continuously analyze logs generated by processes, identifying anomalies and triggering recovery actions when specific error thresholds are met. For example, if an application fails to respond to requests multiple times, the alert system can trigger a script or administrative command to restart the application based on pre-defined policies.

Disaster recovery tools also play a pivotal role in process recovery, particularly for complex applications or those handling sensitive data. Automated backup solutions ensure that critical data is regularly saved and can be restored quickly in the event of a process failure or system crash. Tools like `Bacula` or `rsnapshot` automate the backup process while providing options to recover specific resources, preserving the integrity of operations.

In scenarios involving batch processing or heavy computational tasks, implementing job schedulers can optimize recovery efforts. Tools like `cron` or `at` in Linux can schedule automatic re-execution of tasks that fail. For instance, if a batch job expected to run at 2 AM fails, the script can log this failure, and within the automated job scheduling, retry mechanisms can be initiated at a designated time without manual intervention.

To enhance the robustness of automatic recovery tools, it is prudent to apply a testing protocol that evaluates the effectiveness of these tools periodically. Conducting recovery drills allows administrators to validate that processes restart correctly, data is intact post-recovery, and performance resumes as expected. Documenting these tests and maintaining records of the outcomes helps refine recovery plans and reinforces an organization's readiness to respond to real incidents.

In conclusion, leveraging automatic recovery tools is vital for maintaining resilience and efficiency within Linux processes and services. By embracing process supervision through systemd, utilizing flexible monitoring frameworks like supervisord and monit, integrating orchestration solutions like Kubernetes, and enhancing visibility through logging and alerting systems, administrators can create a safety net for critical applications. Coupling these technologies with robust backup strategies, job schedulers, and regular testing protocols cultivates an environment primed for swift recovery and continuity, significantly reducing the impact of unexpected process failures.

14.4. Failsafes in Process Management

The management of processes is a critical function in Linux system administration, necessitating robust strategies and thorough understanding to ensure system performance and security. In this context, failsafes in process management become a focal point for safeguarding processes against unforeseen issues that can lead to system instability or service interruptions. This subchapter discusses the essential failsafe mechanisms to protect processes and how they can enhance the resilience of Linux environments.

Failsafes in process management can be understood as proactive measures aimed at maintaining operational integrity in the face of potential failures. One of the primary approaches to establishing such failsafes is through meticulous planning of backup processes for quick recovery in case of process failures. Implementing automated backup strategies ensures that critical data or services can be restored promptly, minimizing downtime and the impact on users. Administrators should design a disaster recovery plan emphasizing not only the types of data being backed up but also the frequency of these backups, ensuring data is current and minimizing potential data loss during a crash.

Automating recovery processes can further augment these efforts. This involves employing tools that can automatically detect when a processed fails, triggering a recovery script or operation that reinstates the service with minimal human intervention. For example, systemd's capabilities to monitor service health means that it can automatically restart a service that has failed. This built-in recovery mechanism acts as a failsafe that ensures critical services remain operational even when unexpected issues arise.

Another essential failsafe involves creating process watchdogs—services or scripts that monitor other processes for signs of failure. If a monitored process does not respond within a predefined timeframe, the watchdog can automatically take corrective action, such as restarting the affected service or invoking alert notifications for review. This proactive oversight minimizes the time critical processes remain inactive, improving overall system resilience.

In addition to these monitoring mechanisms, administrators must also implement robust logging practices. Creating detailed logs of process activities, resource usage, and error events aids in troubleshooting and understanding process behavior over time. Centralized logging solutions, such as the ELK stack (Elasticsearch, Logstash, and Kibana), enable the aggregation of logs for efficient analysis. By evaluating these logs, administrators can identify trends or patterns indicative of potential failures before they escalate into critical issues.

Moreover, regularly reviewing and updating process management configurations forms an essential part of the failsafe strategy. The environment in which applications operate can change over time due to updates, new applications, or shifts in user demands. Therefore, periodically assessing the adequacy of current configurations ensures that processes are optimized for available resources and can adapt promptly to changes, diminishing the risk of failures.

On the security front, leveraging technologies such as SELinux or AppArmor enhances failsafe implementations by enforcing strict access controls. These tools can prevent unauthorized process actions that could lead to vulnerabilities or system failures. By employing appropriate security measures, administrators can create a safer environment in which processes operate effectively and securely.

Training users and team members is also a critical aspect of building robust failsafes. By educating users about appropriate resource usage, the importance of reporting unusual behavior, and best practices when creating processes, administrators can foster a culture of awareness and responsibility that contributes to overall system stability.

Finally, conducting post-failure analyses is essential for continuous improvement. After a significant process failure, administrators should evaluate the incident, documenting actions taken, lessons learned, and potential improvements to existing processes. This iterative review can lead to the development of improved failsafe strategies, refining the company's process management approach over time.

In summary, establishing failsafes in process management is vital for ensuring the resilience and stability of Linux systems. By planning and automating recovery processes, employing monitoring tools, creating thorough logging practices, regularly updating configurations, implementing strict security measures, training users, and conducting post-failure assessments, administrators can create a robust framework for managing processes effectively. These failsafe mechanisms not only protect against performance degradation but also enhance confidence in the overall reliability of the Linux environment, allowing it to operate smoothly, much like a finely-tuned machine. As system demands evolve, continual attention to these failsafes will ensure that processes remain protected and nurtured within the ecosystem.

14.5. Preventive Measures and Readiness

In the realm of system administration, preventive measures and readiness stand as pillars supporting robust Linux process management. Establishing a protective framework ensures system stability, enhances resilience against failures, and fosters a culture of proactive oversight. This subchapter delves into essential strategies and practices that administrators can implement to prevent issues before they arise, allowing them to maintain a responsive and efficient operational environment.

Preventive measures begin with thorough documentation and knowledge sharing. Administrators should establish clear guidelines for process management, outlining best practices for process creation, monitoring, and termination. This documentation becomes invaluable, particularly in environments with multiple users and complex interdependencies. Training team members on established protocols and ensuring that everyone understands their roles and responsibilities equips them to contribute actively to system integrity. Regular workshops and training programs can also be organized to keep the team updated on the latest developments and techniques in process management.

Monitoring plays a crucial role in preventive maintenance. Administrators should employ comprehensive monitoring solutions that provide real-time insights into system behavior. Tools such as Nagios, Zabbix, or Prometheus can track vital metrics and generate alerts when predefined thresholds are reached. By continually monitoring CPU usage, memory consumption, I/O operations, and network activity, administrators can identify potential issues early and intervene before they escalate into significant problems. Setting up automated logging systems can also help capture process activities, providing a historical context that can inform future decisions.

Regular audits of system processes and resource allocations are essential preventive measures. Conducting these audits allows administrators to evaluate the effectiveness of current configurations, identify redundant or obsolete processes, and assess whether resource allocations are adequately aligned with user needs. These audits can reveal potential bottlenecks or weaknesses within the process landscape, paving the way for optimized configurations and streamlining operations.

Creating failover and recovery plans ensures that processes can continue operating in the event of unexpected failures. Establishing automatic recovery tools, such as utilizing systemd's built-in capabilities for service supervision, allows administrators to configure services to restart automatically when they fail. Additionally, implementing backup solutions helps preserve critical data—ensuring that services can be restored swiftly without significant downtime during unforeseen incidents. Regularly testing failover procedures and backup restorations further prepares administrators to respond efficiently when emergencies occur.

Another critical preventive measure is to actively maintain and update software dependencies, including system libraries and applications. Keeping packages and libraries up to date mitigates the risk of vulnerabilities that could be exploited, ultimately leading to process failures or system breaches. Automated package management tools like apt, yum, or dnf can facilitate this process, checking for and applying updates as needed while keeping logs of those updates for future reference.

Resource limits and control policies are essential when considering scalability and sustainability. Implementing quotas using control groups (cgroups) ensures that processes are confined to predefined resource limits, reducing the risk of resource starvation. Setting appropriate resource limits—e.g., allocating specific amounts of CPU and memory for particular processes—prevents any single process from overwhelming shared resources, which could degrade system performance.

Engaging in systematic testing and validation allows administrators to assess how processes respond to changes, whether those changes stem from configuration adjustments, new deployments, or system upgrades. This verification fosters confidence in system stability and mitigates the risk of introducing pitfalls during the change management process.

Finally, fostering a proactive culture of continuous improvement among team members is essential. Encouraging all users to take part in identifying potential problems or areas for enhancement creates a collaborative atmosphere. Gathering feedback and insights from various stakeholders can unveil opportunities for process refinement and optimization, allowing the system to adapt and improve continuously.

In conclusion, incorporating preventive measures and readiness into Linux process management can significantly enhance system stability and performance. By establishing comprehensive documentation, employing monitoring solutions, conducting regular audits, creating failover plans, maintaining software dependencies, implementing resource controls, engaging in systematic testing, and fostering a culture of collaboration, administrators can cultivate a resilient operating environment. This readiness prepares organizations to navigate unexpected challenges while ensuring a smooth and efficient operational landscape—creating a thriving ecosystem where processes can flourish and users benefit from robust support. Just as a gardener diligently prepares the soil and environment to foster growth, so too must administrators tend to their systems with care and foresight, ensuring they are primed for success.

15. Virtualization and Containerization Impacts on Processes

15.1. Processes in Virtual Environments

Processes in virtual environments operate under unique constraints and behaviors that impact how system resources are allocated and managed. Understanding these nuances is essential for system administrators who need to ensure that virtualized systems are as responsive and efficient as their physical counterparts. This subchapter delves into the intricacies of managing processes within virtual environments, shedding light on the strategies and techniques needed to optimize performance.

Virtual environments, such as those created by hypervisors (e.g., VMware, KVM, VirtualBox), encapsulate their processes within a defined boundary that separates them from the host system. Each virtual machine (VM) operates with its own operating system and appears as an independent physical machine to the processes running within it. However, this isolation can lead to unique challenges, particularly in resource allocation and performance.

One of the primary considerations when managing processes in virtual environments is understanding how resource allocation differs from that in traditional systems. Resources such as CPU, memory, and storage must be provisioned carefully, as the hypervisor allocates these resources to each VM based on configured settings. As a result, it is crucial to monitor resource usage within VMs to avoid oversubscription, which can lead to contention and degraded performance for all processes running within those confines.

To tackle this, administrators should implement robust monitoring solutions that track the performance of both the host and individual VMs. Tools like Nagios, Zabbix, and Grafana provide valuable insights into CPU usage, memory consumption, and network bandwidth, revealing possible bottlenecks that could impede process performance. For example, if a specific VM consistently consumes high CPU resources, administrators may need to adjust its configuration or allocate more resources to ensure that it performs optimally.

Moreover, understanding the hypervisor's resource management capabilities can help administrators make informed decisions when allocating resources. Most modern hypervisors provide features such as dynamic resource allocation, allowing VMs to request additional CPU or memory on-the-fly based on their current workload. This elasticity is particularly important in virtualized environments with fluctuating loads, as it enables processes to adapt seamlessly to changing demands without manual intervention.

In virtual environments, processes can also be affected by the underlying storage architecture. Disk I/O performance can vary depending on the type of storage used (e.g., SSDs, HDDs), and the manner in which the storage is allocated to VMs. Utilizing techniques like storage thin provisioning can optimize resource usage, allowing multiple VMs to share storage without dedicating physical space unnecessarily. However, this can also lead to performance hits if not managed correctly. Administrators should monitor disk I/O patterns and adjust storage settings to ensure that processes have the necessary bandwidth for optimal performance, especially in environments reliant on database or file system operations.

Networking is another critical aspect of process management in virtual environments. VMs often communicate with one another and the external world through virtual network interfaces, which can introduce latency and bottleneck issues. To address this, employing techniques such as virtual LANs (VLANs) can help segregate and manage network traffic efficiently. Configuring Quality of Service (QoS) policies further assists in prioritizing network traffic and ensuring critical processes receive the necessary bandwidth to perform effectively.

Real-time considerations also come into play when managing processes in virtual environments. Many applications may rely on low-latency communications; thus, understanding the architecture of your virtual networks, including potential overhead introduced by virtual switches and routing, is essential. Fine-tuning these configurations can greatly improve responsiveness and overall performance.

Process isolation within VMs is a fundamental consideration as well. Virtualization inherently provides a level of security through isolation, but additional practices should be implemented to enhance this. Administrators can limit VM capabilities, ensuring that even if one VM is compromised, the exposure to the whole system is minimal. Configuring SELinux or AppArmor profiles for each VM can enforce stricter access control, providing a safeguard against unauthorized resource access.

Lastly, regular updates and maintenance of the hypervisor and guest OS within each VM are integral to maintaining process performance. Outdated packages can introduce vulnerabilities, impact efficiency, or cause compatibility issues that hinder process execution. Employing automation tools for updates can alleviate this burden and help keep process environments secure and optimized.

In conclusion, managing processes in virtual environments requires a comprehensive understanding of resource allocation, monitoring, isolation, and performance optimization. By employing robust monitoring tools, understanding hypervisor capabilities, optimizing storage and networking configurations, and prioritizing security, administrators can enhance process performance in virtualized settings. Just as one cultivates a delicate bonsai, so too must administrators carefully nurture their virtual environments, ensuring each process flourishes optimally within its designated space. With diligent oversight and effective strategies, processes can operate seamlessly, even amidst the complexities introduced by virtualization.

15.2. Optimizing Containers for Process Efficiency

In the evolving field of Linux process management, optimizing containers for process efficiency is an essential consideration for system administrators. Containers provide a lightweight and efficient method for deploying applications, capitalizing on the benefits of isolation and resource management. This subchapter explores the strategies and best practices for tuning container deployments to ensure that processes operate at optimal efficiency.

A foundational aspect of optimizing container efficiency lies in the careful design of container images. Creating minimal images reduces the size and memory footprint of containers, leading to faster startup times and improved resource utilization. Using multi-stage builds in Docker allows administrators to separate the build environment from the production environment, ensuring that only necessary dependencies are included within the final image. This practice not only enhances performance but also helps maintain a more secure and manageable container.

Resource allocation is another critical factor in container optimization. By utilizing features such as Kubernetes resource limits and requests or Docker's built-in CPU and memory limitations, administrators can ensure that each container is allocated an appropriate amount of resources without overcommitting the host. Setting clear resource thresholds enables efficient resource sharing, preventing situations where a single container monopolizes system resources, thereby impacting the performance of others.

Additionally, container orchestration tools like Kubernetes play a vital role in optimizing process efficiency through automated scaling and self-healing capabilities. With horizontal pod autoscalers, Kubernetes can automatically scale the number of container instances up or down based on real-time demand. This adaptive capability ensures that sufficient resources are available during peak usage and minimizes waste during low traffic periods, further enhancing efficiency.

Networking settings also contribute significantly to container performance. By optimizing network configurations and implementing service meshes (like Istio), administrators can streamline communications between services while managing traffic efficiently. Implementing ClusterIP or LoadBalancer services in Kubernetes allows for effective distribution of requests across multiple container instances, minimizing latency and improving overall responsiveness.

Moreover, ensuring that containers run with the least privileges necessary enhances both security and process efficiency. Configuring user permissions within containers through the USER directive or leveraging role-based access controls in Kubernetes ensures that containers do not operate with escalated privileges. This practice limits the potential attack surface and minimizes the risk of resource misuse or unauthorized access.

Monitoring container performance is essential for optimization. Effective use of tools like Prometheus combined with Grafana allows for real-time visibility into container metrics, resource usage, and application performance. By continuously monitoring containers, administrators can quickly identify potential performance bottlenecks, making it easier to troubleshoot and optimize resource allocations as needed.

To facilitate rapid iteration and automation, integrating continuous integration and continuous deployment (CI/CD) practices leads to more efficient container lifecycle management. Incorporating testing frameworks into CI/CD pipelines helps validate application performance within containers early in the development phase, ensuring that processes run efficiently before deployment.

Docker's health check feature allows for assessing the status of a running container. By defining health check commands in the container specification, administrators can ensure that containers are functioning correctly and can take corrective actions or automate recovery processes when necessary.

Finally, documentation is crucial for successful container management. Thorough documentation of best practices, configurations, and troubleshooting guides assists in maintaining consistency and efficiency. This documentation also facilitates knowledge sharing among team members, helping to address container performance issues collaboratively.

In conclusion, optimizing containers for process efficiency requires a comprehensive approach that encompasses image design, resource allocation, orchestration, networking, security, monitoring, automation, and documentation. By implementing these strategies, system administrators can enhance container performance, ensure responsive applications, and maintain an efficient operational environment. This proactive approach to container management fosters a dynamic ecosystem where processes can thrive, much like the care undertaken to nurture a well-formed bonsai tree. As the landscape of container technologies continues to advance, staying attuned to best practices in optimization will be vital in cultivating robust and efficient systems.

15.3. Resource Sharing in Virtual Systems

Resource sharing in virtual systems is a fundamental aspect of modern computing environments, especially in the realm of process management. As we navigate through the intricate landscape of virtualization and resource allocation, understanding how resources are shared among virtual machines (VMs) becomes paramount for system administrators. In a world where efficiency, performance, and cost-effectiveness are essential, optimizing resource sharing can positively impact the productivity of an entire organization.

Virtualization allows multiple virtual machines to run on a single physical host, sharing the underlying hardware resources. Each virtual machine operates independently and has its own operating system, applications, and processes, mimicking the functionality of a physical machine. However, this independence comes with the responsibility of efficient resource allocation and sharing to ensure that all VMs perform optimally without contention for resources.

One of the classic challenges of resource sharing in virtual systems is managing the allocation of CPU, memory, and storage across multiple VMs efficiently. Each VM has unique resource requirements based on the applications running and user demands. For instance, a web server VM may require rapid access to CPU cycles, while a database VM might need a large allocation of memory for optimal performance.

Sufficient resource allocation ensures that these VMs operate effectively without causing degradation in performance across the host.

Using tools like Virtual Machine Manager (virt-manager) or VMware vSphere, administrators can monitor resource usage across VMs actively. These tools provide visibility into how each VM consumes CPU and memory and helps identify any bottlenecks that may arise. Administrators should regularly analyze these usage patterns and be prepared to make adjustments, such as reallocating resources or scaling up the host hardware, to accommodate growing demands.

Resource management extends beyond mere allocation; it also involves prioritization based on workload characteristics. Dedicated resource allocation policies can be established to ensure that critical VMs receive priority during resource contention scenarios. For instance, utilizing Quality of Service (QoS) settings can guarantee that certain VMs maintain bandwidth thresholds or CPU quotas in busy periods, allowing administrators to control how resources are distributed dynamically based on organizational priorities.

Adaptive resource sharing techniques have emerged as valuable methodologies for managing workloads efficiently. Some virtualization platforms allow for dynamic resource adjustments, wherein resources can be allocated or adjusted on-the-fly based on real-time usage. For example, if a certain VM experiences a spike in demand, the virtualization software can automatically allocate additional CPU or memory resources, allowing it to flourish even under heavy loads. Conversely, during downtime or reduced load, resources can be redistributed, optimizing overall utilization across the host.

Another important aspect to consider is the implications of over-provisioning resources versus underprovisioning them. While over-provisioning may seem like a straightforward solution to avoid bottlenecks, it can lead to resource wastage, increased costs, and diminished performance due to competition among processes for scarce resources. On the other hand, underprovisioning can lead to website slowdowns, application errors, or crashes that negatively impact user experience. Finding the right balance is crucial for successful resource sharing.

Security also plays a vital role in resource-sharing strategies. Each virtual machine can represent a potential security boundary. Resource sharing must incorporate multi-tenancy considerations to ensure that malicious actions within one VM do not compromise the data or performance of others. Implementing strict access controls, isolation techniques, and security policies is essential for maintaining the integrity of shared resources within a virtual environment.

In addition, using monitoring and logging solutions helps assess the effectiveness of resource sharing practices. Deploying solutions like Prometheus with Grafana for visualization provides valuable insights into performance metrics, guiding administrators in optimal resource adjustments and sharing strategies. Historical data can inform plans for restructuring resource allocations or even scaling infrastructure.

In conclusion, resource sharing in virtual systems is a multifaceted challenge that requires careful consideration by system administrators. By utilizing virtualization tools, implementing prioritization strategies, adapting to changing workloads, and maintaining stringent security protocols, organizations can ensure that their processes operate efficiently within their virtual environments. This commitment to effective resource sharing cultivates a thriving ecosystem where processes can execute seamlessly, enhancing service delivery and user experience—a well-tended bonsai exhibiting beauty through precision and care, growing in harmony with its surroundings.

15.4. Security and Isolation in Virtual Layers

In today's interconnected world of computing, where performance, security, and resource efficiency are paramount, the orchestration and management of processes requires an in-depth understanding of the dynamic environment in which these processes operate. In this rapidly evolving landscape, the subchapter "Security and Isolation in Virtual Layers" adds a critical layer of insight into process control, focusing on how modern systems leverage virtualization to enhance security through effective isolation and management of processes.

Virtualization technologies have revolutionized the way computing resources are utilized, allowing multiple virtual machines (VMs) or containers to operate simultaneously on a single physical host. This not only maximizes resource efficiency but also establishes isolated environments that limit the impact of individual process failures and security breaches. Understanding this concept is crucial for system administrators aiming to safeguard critical applications while maintaining optimal performance across their systems.

At the heart of security in virtualized environments is the principle of isolation. Processes running within a VM are logically separated from one another, meaning that a compromise in one VM does not directly impact others. This isolation is achieved through the hypervisor layer, which regulates interactions between virtual machines and the underlying physical hardware. By enforcing strict boundaries, administrators can limit the scope of vulnerabilities associated with individual processes, thereby strengthening the security posture of the entire system.

Using technologies such as namespaces, cgroups, and SELinux, administrators can enhance the isolation of processes within virtual environments. Namespaces provide a means to segregate various aspects of the operating system across VMs, allowing each instance to have its own view of things like process IDs, network interfaces, and filesystem hierarchies. This separation not only enhances security but also simplifies management, as processes can be confined to their respective environments without interference.

Control groups (cgroups) play another crucial role in managing processes by enabling resource allocation and limits within virtualized environments. Administrators can define resource constraints for CPU, memory, and I/O usage, ensuring that each VM operates within its designated thresholds. This method prevents a single VM from monopolizing physical resources, thus safeguarding the performance of neighboring processes. Furthermore, by integrating cgroups with monitoring tools, administrators can gain insights into resource consumption across VMs, allowing for effective auditing and potential adjustments before issues arise.

SELinux (Security-Enhanced Linux) and AppArmor add yet another layer of security by enforcing mandatory access controls for processes across the system. By defining policies that govern which resources processes can access, administrators can mitigate the risk of unauthorized actions while maintaining operational flexibility. These security frameworks provide granular control over process capabilities and, when used correctly, significantly reduce the attack surface of the entire environment.

While the advantages of virtualization and isolation are clear, they also introduce challenges that administrators must navigate. Misconfigured environments can lead to security vulnerabilities or issues in process visibility, making it essential to diligently manage policies governing resource usage and access controls. Regular audits and updates to security policies are crucial to ensure that processes maintain their isolation and adhere to security best practices.

Moreover, as organizations adopt hybrid environments, where on-premises systems interact with cloud resources, maintaining consistency in security policies presents additional complexity. Ensuring that processes running in the cloud adhere to the same security protocols as those in local data centers requires careful planning and implementation of cohesive management strategies.

To summarize, security and isolation in virtual layers represent essential components of contemporary process management. By leveraging virtualization technologies, employing strategic isolation techniques such as namespaces and cgroups, and utilizing security frameworks like SELinux and AppArmor, system administrators can enforce stringent controls over processes, ensuring their integrity while maximizing operational efficiency. This proactive approach not only enhances security but also empowers administrators to create resilient, high-performing environments where processes can execute effectively—demonstrating the crucial balance between performance and protection in process management. As organizations continue to navigate evolving technological landscapes, refining these practices will position them for success amidst emerging challenges and opportunities.

15.5. Trends in Virtual Process Management

In the rapidly evolving landscape of process management, particularly within virtualized environments, staying abreast of current trends is vital for system administrators. 'Trends in Virtual Process Management' highlights significant shifts and developments influencing how processes are managed, optimized, and secured in contemporary systems. From advancements in virtualization technologies to the integration of container orchestration and the adoption of automation practices, these trends shape the future of Linux process management and the operational landscape.

One emerging trend is the surge in containerization technologies, primarily driven by the growing popularity of Docker and Kubernetes. Containerization simplifies deploying and managing applications by isolating processes with lightweight environments that include all dependencies. This approach greatly reduces overhead compared to traditional virtual machines while promoting efficient resource utilization. Consequently, processes within containers can be managed more flexibly, allowing for rapid scaling or adjustments based on workload demands. Administrators must frequently update their skill sets to handle the specifics of container management, focusing on strategies for resource allocation and orchestration.

To complement containerization, hybrid cloud architectures are becoming commonplace. Organizations increasingly deploy processes across multiple environments—on-premises, private cloud, and public cloud—requiring a cohesive management approach that allows for seamless integration. The fluidity of processes between these environments calls for robust monitoring and management tools, ensuring that resource allocation, security policies, and performance metrics align across platforms. Organizations leveraging hybrid cloud strategies should prioritize interoperability among their systems and invest in tools that facilitate cross-environment visibility.

Another trend is the heightened emphasis on security within the process management framework. As system complexity increases, so does the risk of security breaches and vulnerabilities. Administrators are adopting practices such as role-based access controls (RBAC) and implementing security policies through tools like SELinux and AppArmor to safeguard processes from unauthorized access. With the rise of malicious threats targeting process vulnerabilities, ensuring processes run within secure confines is a must. This evolving landscape necessitates continuous training and awareness for administrators to stay updated on perceived threats and effective protective measures.

The integration of artificial intelligence (AI) and machine learning (ML) into process management signifies a transformative trend as well. These technologies can automate various aspects of monitoring, decision-making, and resource allocation. For instance, predictive analytics can identify performance bottlenecks before they significantly impact processes based on historical data trends. Leveraging AI/ML-driven insights allows administrators to make more informed resource allocation decisions dynamically, enhancing efficiency while minimizing manual oversight.

In addition, automation practices are increasingly embraced as businesses seek to improve efficiency and reduce operational costs. Automating routine tasks—such as monitoring, scaling, and adjusting process priorities—frees administrators to focus on critical strategic initiatives. The adoption of Infrastructure as Code (IaaC) principles facilitates automated deployments, ensuring processes are provisioned consistently according to predefined configurations, thereby streamlining operations and shortening deployment cycles.

Real-time performance monitoring is more critical than ever in this context, as it aids in understanding the current and predictive states of processes. Implementing comprehensive monitoring solutions allows administrators to track resource utilization dynamically and identify emerging trends, facilitating timely adjustments. Tools such as Prometheus and Grafana are increasingly employed to visualize performance metrics and integrate alerts, empowering administrators to respond to emerging issues more proactively.

Finally, as organizations navigate the implications of remote work and distributed teams, ensuring that processes are accessible and manageable from various locations becomes increasingly critical. This trend necessitates cloud solutions that allow for remote monitoring, management, and scaling of processes while maintaining security and compliance.

In conclusion, trends in virtual process management reflect the ongoing evolution of technology and its implications for administrators. From embracing containerization and hybrid cloud strategies to enhancing security, automating tasks, and leveraging AI insights, these trends shape the future of Linux process management. As the landscape continues to shift, administrators must remain adaptable, enhancing their skills and implementing best practices to cultivate efficient, secure, and responsive environments. By staying in tune with these trends, administrators can position themselves effectively to meet the demands of modern computing and foster the resilience necessary to navigate challenges ahead.

16. Diagnostics and Troubleshooting Techniques

16.1. Common Process Issues and Resolutions

In the context of Linux process management, understanding and resolving common process issues is critical for maintaining a smooth and efficient operating environment. This section delves into typical problems encountered by system administrators and outlines practical resolutions that can be employed to mitigate these challenges.

One of the most common process issues is resource contention, where multiple processes vie for the same CPU, memory, or I/O resources. This contention can lead to degraded performance, slow response times, and, in some cases, process failures. To resolve this, administrators can monitor CPU usage with commands like 'top' or 'htop' to identify processes consuming excessive resources. Once identified, they can adjust process priorities using the `nice` or `renice` commands to lower the urgency of non-critical processes, allowing more important applications to perform optimally.

Another frequent issue arises from misbehaving or rogue processes that consume excessive memory due to memory leaks or inefficient code. This can lead to the system using swap space more frequently, resulting in performance degradation. The first step in addressing high memory usage is to analyze the offending process using tools like `ps`, `pmap`, or `smem` to understand its memory consumption. If the memory usage is consistent and abnormal, it may be necessary to log the process actions, investigate the application code, and ultimately restart or kill the process while corrective measures are put in place.

Disk I/O bottlenecks also present challenges for process management, particularly in data-intensive applications. Processes that engage in excessive read/write operations can lead to increased latency and reduced throughput. To diagnose and resolve I/O slowness, tools like `iotop` or `iostat` can help pinpoint which processes are responsible. Administrators can consider implementing disk I/O limits using cgroups to prevent one process from monopolizing disk access or optimize the application code to reduce unnecessary I/O operations.

Networking issues can also hinder process efficiency, especially in environments using distributed applications. Latency, packet loss, or bottlenecked network interfaces can result in sluggish responses or dropped connections. Monitoring tools such as `iftop`, `netstat`, and `ping` can help diagnose network-related problems. If a specific process regularly encounters network issues, adjusting socket buffer sizes and applying TCP tuning parameters may help improve network performance.

Sometimes, processes may display erratic behavior due to conflicting dependencies or library versions. Maintaining consistent environments is vital for ensuring that processes operate smoothly. Using tools like `ldd`, administrators should track shared libraries that processes depend upon. If discrepancies are identified, reinstalling missing libraries or updating them to compatible versions may resolve issues related to dependency conflicts.

Automatic restarts can also be a key aspect of resolving process issues. Using monitoring and process management tools like `systemd`, `supervisord`, or `monit`, administrators can configure processes to automatically restart upon failure. This proactive strategy minimizes downtime and preserves performance, allowing critical services to remain accessible to users.

Finally, ensuring proper documentation of process management practices and common issues faced can provide a valuable reference for addressing problems quickly in the future. Providing a clear set of guidelines for troubleshooting and resolution can expedite support efforts and improve operational efficiency.

In summary, effectively managing common process issues in Linux entails continuous monitoring, quick identification of resource usage anomalies, and the implementation of practical solutions to mitigate challenges. By adopting a systematic approach to analyzing and resolving issues—whether through prioritization, resource limitations, monitoring, or automatic restarts—administrators can maintain a high-performing and stable environment. Embracing these practices helps cultivate a responsive Linux system where processes operate efficiently, much like a meticulously pruned bonsai thriving under careful stewardship.

16.2. Scripting for Problem Detection

In any operating system, managing process errors and performance issues is a critical responsibility for system administrators. Scripting for problem detection plays a vital role in proactively identifying and addressing these challenges, enabling systems to run smoothly even under varying workloads. By automating processes that monitor system behavior, administrators can quickly respond to anomalies, ensuring minimal disruptions.

To effectively script for problem detection, the first step involves defining clear objectives. This might include monitoring specific resource thresholds, tracking process statuses, or identifying abnormal behaviors. For instance, an administrator might want to detect processes that exceed a certain CPU or memory allocation, or those that enter unexpected states, such as stalled or terminated unexpectedly.

Bash scripts, which are commonly used in Linux environments, provide a powerful tool for implementing these monitoring and detection mechanisms. Below is an example of a basic script that alerts the administrator when a specified process exceeds predetermined CPU usage:

```
\#!/bin/bash

THRESHOLD=80  \# Define CPU usage threshold
PROCESS_NAME="my_process" \# Specify the process to monitor

\# Check the CPU usage of the specified process
CPU_USAGE=$(ps -C "$PROCESS_NAME" -o %cpu=)

\# Compare CPU usage to the threshold
```

```
if [ "$(echo "$CPU_USAGE > $THRESHOLD" | bc)" -eq 1 ]; then
    echo "Alert: $PROCESS_NAME is using $CPU_USAGE% CPU,
which exceeds the threshold!"
    \# Additional actions can be taken, like sending an
alert email
fi
```

This script checks the CPU usage of a defined process and compares it against the set threshold, providing a crucial early warning to administrators. Once a script identifies such an issue, administrators can respond accordingly by adjusting process priorities, redistributing workloads, or analyzing the underlying causes of the spike.

Moreover, leveraging advanced monitoring tools can enhance scripting capabilities further. Solutions such as Nagios, Zabbix, or Prometheus can integrate scripting functionalities to monitor process statuses and resource usage continually. They allow for configuring alerts based on defined metrics, paving the way for rapid responses to issues detected through automated testing scripts.

In addition to monitoring CPU and memory usage, administrators should also implement scripts to detect other potential errors, such as I/O bottlenecks or problematic exit statuses of critical processes. By checking logs and regularly evaluating application health through tailored scripts, system performance can be kept under constant review.

Incorporating diagnostic logging into the scripting process also enriches problem detection. Structured logging allows administrators to track process activities over time, enabling more nuanced analysis during troubleshooting. When a scripted analysis highlights an anomaly, the logs provide context for understanding the series of events that led to the issue.

Another best practice lies in developing a framework for regularly scheduled script runs. Utilizing tools like cron can automate the execution of monitoring scripts at specified intervals, ensuring continuous oversight of process performance and health. By setting scripts to run frequently, administrators gain a comprehensive view of system behavior over time, allowing for timely evaluations of performance trends.

Moreover, sharing findings with stakeholders can enhance collaborative troubleshooting efforts. Sharing reports generated by monitoring scripts or aggregating logs provides insight that can inform development teams about potential inefficiencies or areas for improvement within applications, aiding overall operational efficiency.

In conclusion, scripting for problem detection is a powerful strategy for maintaining process efficiency and performance in Linux systems. By implementing tailored scripts that monitor resource usage, structured logging practices, scheduled executions, and effective stakeholder communication, administrators can proactively identify issues and streamline processes. Emphasizing automated detection mechanisms allows for a more resilient environment where processes can flourish and adapt to changing workloads, mirroring the meticulous nurturing required to cultivate and maintain a thriving bonsai tree. As organizations continue to evolve, system administrators who harness the power of scripting for monitoring will be better positioned to maintain stable and efficient Linux environments.

16.3. Advanced Troubleshooting Tools

Advanced Troubleshooting Tools play a crucial role in managing and optimizing processes within a Linux environment. These tools enable administrators to diagnose issues effectively, analyze system performance, and ultimately enhance the resilience of applications. A well-equipped arsenal of troubleshooting tools maximizes efficiency while minimizing downtime, enabling seamless operations even under fluctuating situations.

At the forefront of advanced troubleshooting tools is the command-line utility `perf`. Designed for performance analysis, `perf` helps to monitor system capabilities and measure CPU performance counters. It provides rich insights into what processes are consuming CPU cycles and where bottlenecks may arise. Leveraging `perf`, administrators can view detailed reports on CPU utilization, cache misses, context switches, and more, allowing deeper diagnostics beyond what standard monitoring tools provide.

Another highly regarded tool for troubleshooting is `strace`. By tracing system calls made by processes, `strace` allows administrators to see what a process is doing in real time, including file accesses, network connections, and memory operations. This visibility is invaluable for diagnosing issues with specific applications, as it helps illuminate the underlying causes of abnormal behavior or failures. Utilizing `strace` effectively requires an understanding of how applications interact with the OS, making it a powerful diagnostic tool for seasoned administrators.

For identifying memory-related problems, `valgrind` is an exceptional tool that helps in detecting memory leaks, invalid memory accesses, and buffer overflows in applications. By running applications under `valgrind`, administrators can gain insights into memory usage patterns and identify specific leaks or errors, facilitating the optimization of process memory management.

In systems where I/O performance is critical, `iotop` is an invaluable tool that provides real-time monitoring of disk I/O usage across processes. This tool helps identify which processes are consuming the most I/O resources, guiding administrators in troubleshooting performance bottlenecks associated with disk operations. Coupled with tools like `iostat`, which provides I/O statistics along with utilization metrics, administrators can maintain a focused approach to improve overall performance.

Network performance can also present challenges, and tools such as `tcpdump` and `iftop` are essential for diagnosing network-related issues affecting process performance. `tcpdump` allows for capturing and analyzing packets traversing the network, providing valuable insights into how processes communicate. `iftop`, on the other hand, provides dynamic bandwidth monitoring, allowing administrators to assess which processes are generating the most network load.

Often overlooked is the importance of logging systems in advanced troubleshooting. Tools like `rsyslog`, `syslog-ng`, or the systemd journal can aggregate logs from various sources, providing a centralized view of process activities, error messages, and warnings. By collecting these logs, administrators can correlate system events and use them to diagnose issues more effectively. Analyzing logs post-incident can provide vital information detailing the sequence of events leading to a failure, thereby informing future preventive strategies.

Automated diagnostics can significantly enhance troubleshooting efforts. By scripting monitoring and recovery actions, administrators can create custom tools that act upon specific failure conditions. Utilizing languages like Bash, Python, or Perl, scripts can be built to automate critical checks, alert the administrator on certain thresholds, or even take corrective actions without manual intervention. Automation reduces reliance on constant supervision, freeing up resources for more strategic tasks.

Integrating visual dashboard tools such as Grafana, which can compile data from various monitoring sources, offers admins a bird's eye view of system performance. These dashboards can visualize CPU, memory, and I/O metrics meaningfully, allowing administrators to identify trends and anomalies quickly. With data visualization, troubleshooting shifts from reactive to proactive, enabling quicker identification of emerging issues.

Finally, fostering a collaborative culture among administrators and developers enhances troubleshooting efficiency. Engaging in discussions around recurring issues, sharing insights from performance audits, and collectively brainstorming solutions can lead to innovative approaches to process management.

In conclusion, advanced troubleshooting tools in a Linux environment is integral to maintaining system efficiency and stability. By utilizing tools such as `perf`, `strace`, `valgrind`, `iotop`, `tcpdump`, and effective logging systems, administrators can diagnose and resolve issues within processes swiftly. Moreover, automating diagnostics and leveraging visualization tools enhances proactive management, facilitating rapid identification and resolution of potential issues. By fostering a culture of collaboration and knowledge-sharing among team members, organizations can cultivate a resilient operational environment, ensuring that processes thrive under a well-managed framework for performance and stability.

16.4. Logs and Error Reporting

Logs and Error Reporting is a critical component of effective process management within Linux systems. It encompasses the systematic capture, analysis, and reporting of logged events that can indicate process behavior, errors, or system anomalies. By leveraging logs effectively, administrators can diagnose issues, track system performance, and improve application reliability.

At the heart of logs and error reporting lies the concept of structured logging, which involves recording process activities with specific information about their state, resource usage, and errors. The Linux environment offers several logging facilities to assist administrators in this endeavor, with system logging services such as `syslog`, `rsyslog`, or the modern `journalctl` included with Systemd providing robust support for capturing logs.

Effective logging begins with the configuration of appropriate logging levels for processes. Each process can generate log messages categorized by severity, such as debug, info, warning, error, and critical. By tailoring logging levels, administrators can filter out unnecessary verbosity while ensuring critical issues are highlighted for timely attention. For example, a web server might log different types of messages based on its operations, allowing for immediate identification of errors as they occur.

Additionally, processes often log events to different files or destinations based on their configurations. Configuring a centralized logging solution can streamline monitoring and enable the aggregation of logs from multiple sources. Solutions like the ELK Stack (Elasticsearch, Logstash, and Kibana) or Graylog allow administrators to collect, index, and visualize logs in real-time, enabling more efficient error detection and reporting.

Once error logs are captured and consolidated, the next step is to analyze them for meaningful insights. Regular monitoring of logs helps administrators identify recurring errors, performance degradation, or anomalous behaviors among processes. By implementing automated alerting tools that notify when processes generate critical errors, organizations can respond swiftly, minimizing downtime and maintaining operational integrity.

Another key strategy in logs and error reporting involves creating a framework for structured reporting. Regularly scheduled reports summarizing log activities can help administrators monitor trends, identify potential areas for improvement, and refine operational processes. These reports can guide strategic decisions regarding resource allocation, process optimization, and overall system health.

In addition to internal logging systems, leveraging third-party monitoring solutions can enhance error reporting capabilities. Integrating cloud-based monitoring tools can provide more sophisticated analysis and reporting, including the ability to capture metrics over time, generate alerts based on complex conditions, and visualize log data to identify trends.

Furthermore, automatic processes for log rotation and archival are essential in managing log files effectively. Configuring log rotation prevents excessive disk usage by ensuring that logs do not grow indefinitely, while archiving maintains historical records for compliance and analysis. Administrators can employ tools such as `logrotate` to manage log files easily, establishing policies regarding frequency and retention.

In terms of security, logs serve as valuable audit trails that help in incident detection and response. By implementing secure logging practices such as log integrity checks and access controls, administrators can safeguard log data from tampering and unauthorized access.

Ensuring that logs are protected is essential, especially in environments handling sensitive data or critical applications.

Training teams to understand the significance of logs and error reporting enhances their ability to maintain system reliability. Educating users on how to properly configure logs, interpret log messages, and respond to alerts creates a culture of awareness and proactive monitoring.

In conclusion, logs and error reporting form an integral part of process management within Linux systems. By establishing structured logging practices, utilizing centralized logging solutions, implementing automated reporting, creating frameworks for analysis, and ensuring security measures are in place, administrators can cultivate an environment where processes operate efficiently, and issues are detected and resolved promptly. This commitment to robust logging practices fosters a resilient operational space, echoing the meticulous care involved in nurturing a bonsai—each log serving as a vital node in the complex ecosystem of process management. By harnessing logs and error reporting effectively, system administrators can ensure the health and stability of their systems while enhancing overall performance.

16.5. Building a Diagnostic Framework

In any comprehensive exploration of Linux process management, the subchapter on building a diagnostic framework is pivotal. This framework serves as a structured approach to identifying, analyzing, and resolving issues within a Linux environment, thereby enhancing system reliability and performance. Just as a well-crafted framework might support a robust structure in architecture, a diagnostic framework facilitates effective responses to process-related anomalies, making it an invaluable tool for system administrators.

A compelling diagnostic framework begins with clearly defined objectives. Administrators must identify which types of issues are likely to occur within their environments and what the critical metrics are for evaluating performance. This can include resource usage (CPU, memory, I/O), process states, and inter-process dependencies. By establishing key performance indicators (KPIs), administrators can create a baseline against which they can measure potential issues and effectively respond to deviations.

Monitoring tools are the backbone of any solid diagnostic framework. Utilizing tools such as `top`, `htop`, `ps`, `vmstat`, and specialized performance monitoring solutions allows for real-time insights into system performance. These tools should be configured to gather and present relevant data on a continuous basis, enabling quick recognition of performance dips or processes consuming excessive resources. This proactive monitoring allows administrators to detect issues before they escalate into critical failures.

Alongside real-time monitoring, logging becomes an essential component of the diagnostic framework. Logs offer a historical perspective on system activity and alerts administrators to issues post-factum. Implementing robust logging solutions, such as `syslog` or `journald`, facilitates the aggregation of log data across processes, providing invaluable context during troubleshooting. All logs should be regularly reviewed to identify patterns or anomalies that may indicate underlying issues, and retention policies should be established so that logs do not fill available storage unnecessarily.

When designing a diagnostic framework, it is also vital to incorporate a systematic troubleshooting process. This process should outline step-by-step procedures that administrators follow when diagnosing specific problems. For instance, if a service experiences downtime, administrators should first check the service status with `systemctl`, inspect logs with `journalctl`, and examine any error messages. By establishing standard operating procedures for common issues, organizations can streamline their troubleshooting efforts, retaining institutional knowledge that ensures consistency.

Another crucial aspect is the use of automation within the framework. Automation can dramatically enhance the diagnostic process by continuously monitoring systems and generating alerts when predefined thresholds are crossed. Scripting automated tasks that collect diagnostic data upon service failure can also facilitate rapid response times. Using a combination of cron jobs for periodic checks and alerting systems—like Nagios or Prometheus—ensures that administrators are aware of issues in real-time.

In terms of collaboration, building an effective diagnostic framework requires input from various stakeholders in the organization. Engaging application developers, infrastructure specialists, and end-users in discussions about potential bottlenecks and recurring issues can uncover insights that enhance the framework's efficacy. This collaborative approach ensures that the diagnostic framework addresses the unique needs and challenges posed by different processes and applications within the environment.

As new technologies and methods for process management continue to evolve, so too should the diagnostic framework. Regular assessments and updates are vital to ensuring its relevance and effectiveness in a changing landscape. Retaining flexibility within the framework allows administrators to adopt new tools and practices as needed, thereby enhancing its effectiveness.

In conclusion, building a diagnostic framework for process management in Linux is an essential practice for ensuring system reliability and efficiency. By establishing clear objectives, utilizing robust monitoring and logging tools, implementing systematic troubleshooting steps, embracing automation, promoting collaboration, and continually adapting to changes, administrators can ensure a responsive and accountable process management system. This approach not only enhances the operational integrity of Linux environments but also fosters a culture of continuous improvement that meets the demands of modern computing, much like a well-structured building stands resilient against the elements. Ultimately, a solid diagnostic framework provides the necessary support for maintaining a flourishing Linux ecosystem, allowing processes to run efficiently and effectively while safeguarding system stability and security.

17. Scaling Process Management for Enterprise Systems

17.1. System Scaling Considerations

In the context of system scaling considerations, it is crucial to acknowledge how complexities inherent in managing processes evolve as systems grow in size and function. Scaling process management effectively not only enhances performance but also ensures that systems remain responsive under increasing loads. This subchapter will delve into the strategic considerations for scaling process management in enterprise systems, focusing on features such as resource allocation, load balancing, automated recovery, and collaboration.

When scaling process management, one must first assess the existing architecture and determine its limitations. Understanding the current capacity of both hardware and software components is essential for identifying bottlenecks before they become substantial issues. Administrators should employ monitoring tools that provide insights into resource utilization trends over time. This data-driven approach allows for informed decisions regarding when and how to expand capacities, be it through adding resources or optimizing existing workflows.

Effective resource allocation becomes particularly vital in scaling environments. In enterprise systems, resources—such as CPU, memory, and network bandwidth—must be distributed thoughtfully among various processes to prevent performance degradation. Implementing control groups (cgroups) allows administrators to allocate specific resources based on the needs of different applications. These allocations can adapt to changing workloads, ensuring that critical processes receive the resources they require while also managing lower-priority tasks efficiently.

Load balancing is another cornerstone of effectively scaling process management. As user requests and data transactions grow, distributing workloads evenly across available resources becomes imperative. Employing load balancing solutions—whether through hardware appliances or software configurations—enables administrators to manage incoming requests efficiently. For instance, using algorithms like least-connections or round-robin ensures that resources are never overwhelmed, guaranteeing stable performance as demand fluctuates.

Automation also plays a critical role in scaling process management. Automating repetitive tasks not only accelerates processes but also reduces the potential for human error. Tools such as Ansible, Puppet, or Kubernetes can automate deployments, scaling, and configuration management, ensuring that processes maintain peak performance without significant administrative overhead. By integrating automation into the scaling strategy, administrators can focus more on strategic initiatives rather than routine operations.

In addition, incorporating load testing methodologies can offer valuable insights into how processes behave under varying loads. By simulating different usage scenarios, administrators can identify threshold limits and establish robust scaling configurations. This proactive approach allows for the anticipation of resource demands and makes it easier to implement adjustments before performance issues arise.

Collaboration across teams also influences successful scaling efforts. Engaging with developers, operations staff, and other stakeholders promotes a holistic understanding of how each team can contribute to process management scalability. Sharing insights into application performance and resource needs can guide a collective approach to optimization, leading to better outcomes for the entire organization.

As enterprises increasingly adopt cloud-based solutions, leveraging cloud resources plays a significant part in scaling process management. Cloud services allow businesses to dynamically allocate resources based on real-time demand, ensuring that processes operate efficiently regardless of fluctuations. Understanding cloud architecture becomes essential, as it can differ substantially from traditional on-premises setups.

Finally, establishing robust documentation practices helps facilitate successful scaling. Clearly documenting resource configurations, performance benchmarks, and load testing results creates a valuable reference for future scaling efforts. This documentation fosters knowledge sharing within teams and can guide responses to issues as they arise, contributing to improved operational resilience.

In conclusion, scaling process management for enterprise systems involves a multifaceted approach that incorporates effective resource allocation, load balancing, automation, collaboration, testing methodologies, and robust documentation. By embracing these strategies, system administrators can enhance the performance and efficiency of processes, ensuring that enterprise systems remain responsive and resilient even as demands increase. Ultimately, the pursuit of excellence in process management parallels the delicate balance required in a thriving ecosystem, where each element operates harmoniously to support overall success.

17.2. Enterprise Level Pruning Strategies

In the vast and intricate landscape of enterprise-level computing, managing processes efficiently is pivotal to ensuring optimal performance and system integrity. As organizations scale and embrace the complexities of multitasking environments, the necessity for sophisticated and transparent pruning strategies cannot be overstated. This section metaphorically parallels the meticulous practice of bonsai cultivation—where every branch is carefully trimmed to enhance both form and function. Thus, we delve deep into enterprise-level pruning strategies that are essential for optimizing Linux process management.

First and foremost, it is crucial to maintain an accurate and comprehensive understanding of the current process landscape. Within Enterprise Linux systems, tools such as 'top', 'htop', and 'ps' provide necessary insights into process states, resource consumption, and their interdependencies. Regular assessments using these monitoring tools can reveal processes that are consuming disproportionate amounts of CPU, memory, or I/O operations. With this knowledge in hand, administrators can strategically identify processes that require pruning, ensuring that critical applications remain responsive while minimizing the burden of unnecessary or stagnant processes.

One of the effective strategies is to classify processes based on their relevance to the organization's objectives. High-priority processes that directly contribute to core business functions should be managed and preserved rigorously, while processes that are either obsolete or redundant can be scheduled for termination. Creating a robust process classification scheme facilitates prioritization and resource allocation strategy, allowing businesses to focus their efforts where they matter most while streamlining operations.

Implementing resource control mechanisms is also vital for enterprise-level pruning. Control groups (cgroups) enable administrators to set resource limits on processes, ensuring that no single app monopolizes CPU or memory resources that could otherwise support critical enterprise functions. Through enforcing stringent resource usage policies, organizations maintain a healthier process flow, allowing essential applications to run smoothly while constraining those processes that lack operational significance.

Adaptive load balancing approaches further enhance process management across enterprise systems. Utilizing load balancers, administrators can dynamically allocate workloads based on real-time usage patterns. By distributing incoming requests evenly across available resources, load balancing minimizes the risks of individual resource overload and enhances overall responsiveness. This method works symbiotically with process pruning, as processes that are deemed less critical can be offloaded or terminated based on current demand.

Establishing automated scripting for frequent or routine visibility checks can streamline the pruning process further. Automating audits and reviews ensures that systems are continuously analyzed for underutilized or rogue processes. For example, routine scripts can monitor active processes and log resource consumption, generating alerts for any process that exceeds predetermined thresholds. Armed with this data, administrators can efficiently respond to issues before they escalate.

Moreover, leveraging the role of containers within enterprise architectures can optimize process management. Containers encapsulate application dependencies and provide isolation while sharing the same underlying OS. By utilizing container orchestration platforms like Kubernetes, organizations can manage hundreds of containerized applications simultaneously, simplifying the process of scaling, updating, and pruning applications within virtual environments.

Incorporating systematic feedback from users is another vital aspect. Engaging the end-users and developers in dialogs regarding active processes not only allows technical teams to align priorities but also creates a flexible process management culture. Users can provide invaluable insights into which applications experience performance issues, enabling quicker decision-making and process adjustments.

Finally, documenting and sharing lessons learned from previous pruning operations creates a knowledge base that aids continual improvement. After significant pruning activities, conducting reviews to analyze the fallout—whether successful or not—can drive future strategies, instilling a culture of continual growth and adaptation within the organization.

In conclusion, enterprise-level pruning strategies for Linux process management involve a synergy of active monitoring, resource control, adaptive load balancing, automation, user engagement, and documentation. By integrating these practices, organizations can streamline their processes, retain critical operational capabilities, and ensure that their systems run efficiently and responsively. Through methodical pruning, akin to the precise cultivation of a bonsai, enterprise systems can refine their processes to flourish within their environments, attaining unprecedented levels of performance and resilience while facing the ever-evolving technological landscape.

17.3. Integrating Process Management Across Platforms

In large-scale Linux environments, the integration of process management across disparate platforms is an increasingly vital topic for system administrators who strive to ensure seamless operations and efficient resource allocation. Just as the branches of a thriving bonsai tree connect and interact while retaining their unique characteristics, effectively synchronizing process workflows across diverse systems can enhance overall organizational agility and responsiveness.

The first step in integrating process management across platforms involves establishing a consistent set of protocols and methodologies. Administrators should define clear standards for process behaviors, resource allocations, and performance metrics across the various systems they manage. This ensures that each platform adheres to established best practices, minimizing discrepancies that could lead to inefficient operations. By implementing uniform policies, organizations create a standardized language for managing processes, making collaboration across teams more effective and reducing confusion.

Next, leveraging robust automation tools can significantly enhance the integration process. Tools such as Ansible, Puppet, or Chef can be employed to orchestrate process management actions across multiple platforms. By describing the desired states of systems in configuration files, administrators can automate tasks related to process management—such as deploying applications, adjusting resource allocations, and managing network configurations—regardless of the underlying infrastructure. This automation fosters a more streamlined process management approach, allowing teams to maintain consistency and focus on higher-level objectives.

Effective communication between processes in different environments is another critical aspect. Implementing APIs or message queuing systems can facilitate seamless interaction across platforms, promoting integration between heterogeneous processes. By using standard protocols (such as RESTful APIs) for process communication, organizations can ensure that different systems can exchange data and function collaboratively without the pitfalls of platform constraints. This capability is especially pivotal when dealing with microservices architectures, where services must communicate and coordinate with various processes.

Data synchronization is also crucial when integrating processes across platforms. Organizations may employ distributed databases or data replication strategies to ensure that processes running on different systems can access up-to-date information. Utilizing technologies such as Apache Kafka or RabbitMQ facilitates interoperability, allowing systems to send messages and share data effectively. By ensuring that all relevant processes are aware of the latest data changes, organizations can reduce errors and enhance overall efficiency.

Moreover, monitoring becomes critical in ensuring that process integrations perform as expected. Employing centralized monitoring solutions to oversee processes across various systems allows administrators to gain insights into performance and identify bottlenecks quickly. By using tools like Prometheus with Grafana dashboards, organizations can visualize metrics from multiple platforms, ensuring holistic visibility that supports informed decision-making.

In addition, training and collaboration between teams are essential for successful integration. Ensuring that team members are aware of each platform's unique characteristics and capabilities encourages cooperation while streamlining processes. Establishing regular cross-platform meetings or training sessions can foster a shared understanding, allowing teams to share insights about process interactions and performance optimizations.

As organizations increasingly adopt cloud services, integrating process management within hybrid environments becomes paramount. Flexibility in resource allocation, scaling strategies, and elastic workloads allows enterprises to respond dynamically to changing demands. Administrators must focus on utilizing tools that handle cloud-native architectures while maintaining process control and visibility.

Finally, while integrating processes across platforms is essential, organizations must also factor in security considerations. Establishing a unified security policy for processes operating in different environments mitigates the risk of vulnerabilities that could arise from inadequate oversight. By enforcing consistent security practices—such as employing agile container security measures or implementing access controls using identity and access management (IAM) frameworks—organizations can enhance protection across platforms.

In conclusion, integrating process management across diverse platforms is crucial for optimizing overall operational efficiency in large-scale Linux environments. By creating standardized processes, leveraging automation tools, facilitating communication, ensuring data accessibility, monitoring performance, fostering collaboration, adapting to cloud services, and implementing robust security measures, organizations can ensure that their processes work harmoniously across varying environments. This meticulous integration—much like the delicate dance of branches in a bonsai tree—enables enterprises to thrive in a complex, interconnected digital ecosystem, supporting agile and responsive structures that meet evolving business needs. As systems evolve, the integration strategies will be essential for maintaining flexibility and resilience against future challenges.

17.4. Risk Management in Large Scale Process Handling

Risk management in large scale process handling encompasses strategies and mechanisms to mitigate potential issues that arise from the complexities and interdependencies of numerous concurrent processes operating within systems, especially in a Linux environment. As organizations grow and scale their operations, the intricacies of managing processes can introduce significant risks that, if left unaddressed, may lead to performance degradation, security vulnerabilities, or system failures.

To begin with, it's crucial to identify potential risks in large-scale process environments. These can include resource contention where multiple processes strive for limited CPU, memory, or I/O bandwidth, leading to performance bottlenecks. The potential for unresponsive processes, cascading failures due to interdependencies, and the complexity of managing numerous configurations also heightens risk. Regular audits and monitoring for system performance using tools like 'top', 'htop', and 'vmstat' help identify these risks early, allowing for proactive management before they escalate into critical failures.

One of the essential strategies for risk management is resource allocation and load balancing. Ensuring that resources are assigned equitably among processes minimizes the chances of contention. Load balancers that distribute workloads evenly across multiple servers or instances prevent situations where system overload can occur, while tools like Kubernetes smartly manage resource allocations for containerized processes, automatically scaling resources up or down in response to current demands. The implementation of control groups (cgroups) can also restrain the resource usage of specific processes, reducing the risk of any single task overwhelming system capabilities.

Effective process isolation is another crucial aspect of risk management. By segregating processes within containers or utilizing namespaces, administrators minimize the fallout of process failures. In the event that malicious activity arises within one process, isolation prevents it from affecting others, thus protecting system integrity. When combined with strict access controls and security measures such as SELinux, process isolation becomes even more robust, allowing for enhanced security among processes.

Another critical component of risk management is failure recovery mechanisms. Implementing automatic recovery tools such as systemd's built-in service recovery options, supervisord, or Kubernetes' self-healing features allows processes to resume operation quickly after a failure. Such automation minimizes downtime and ensures that recovery actions are consistently applied without manual oversight. In conjunction with these mechanisms, administrators should maintain clear practices for backup and disaster recovery, preserving valuable data and configurations to prevent data loss during critical failures.

Furthermore, establishing a culture of continuous improvement and documentation within the organization aids in identifying potential risks. Documenting past incidents, responses, and resolutions creates a knowledge base that can be referenced for future risk assessments and management strategies. This historical data can provide insights into recurring issues and help refine practices for addressing them more effectively.

Risk management also involves collaborating across teams. Engaging developers and users in understanding workload patterns and potential bottlenecks enhances communication regarding resource needs. Regular cross-team meetings or feedback sessions can surface valuable insights into process management and performance optimization, ultimately informing better decision-making.

Finally, administrators need to prepare for unforeseen challenges, particularly with the ever-evolving landscape of technology. Staying abreast of emerging risks associated with new technologies—including cloud, containers, and microservices—allows administrators to implement appropriate risk management strategies tailored to these challenges. By continuously educating themselves on the latest trends and best practices in process management, administrators can fortify their systems against potential vulnerabilities.

In conclusion, risk management in large-scale process handling within Linux entails a comprehensive approach that includes identifying potential risks, ensuring effective resource allocation, employing process isolation, implementing automated recovery mechanisms, fostering continuous improvement, collaborating across teams, and preparing for unforeseen challenges. By employing these strategies, administrators maintain systems that can adapt to varying demands while ensuring operational stability, security, and efficiency. This vigilant approach mirrors the diligence required in the meticulous art of bonsai cultivation—balancing the needs of each process within the environment while nurturing overall growth and resilience.

17.5. Case Studies in Scalability Success

In the realm of system administration, case studies serve as invaluable repositories of knowledge and experience, highlighting the real-world application of concepts in scalability success. The following examples showcase how organizations have navigated the complexities of scaling their processes within Linux environments, ultimately enhancing performance, resource management, and overall system reliability.

One prominent case study involves a multinational e-commerce platform faced with challenges related to sudden spikes in user traffic during seasonal sales events. As the number of concurrent users surged, present infrastructure was incapable of handling the load, resulting in degraded performance, slow response times, and higher rates of cart abandonment. To address these scalability challenges, the company implemented an agile approach, adopting a containerized microservices architecture using Docker and Kubernetes.

The initial phase involved decomposing monolithic applications into microservices, where each service handled distinct business functions (e.g., inventory management, payment processing, and customer authentication). This modular approach allowed for more precise scaling—enabling individual services to be scaled up or down based on demand. During subsequent sales events, the organization utilized Kubernetes' Horizontal Pod Autoscaler, which automatically adjusted the number of running pods (containers) based on real-time metrics like CPU and memory usage. This adaptive capacity proved successful, as it optimized resource allocation without human intervention, simultaneously maintaining application performance and user satisfaction.

Additionally, the company integrated load balancing strategies through Nginx, distributing incoming user requests fairly across available service instances. This not only prevented any single instance from becoming overwhelmed but ensured high availability, effectively mitigating impacts during peak demand periods. Real-time monitoring tools like Prometheus and Grafana provided valuable insights into system behavior, allowing the organization to detect potential bottlenecks in real time and adjust configurations promptly, resulting in vastly improved scalability and resilience.

The second case study involves a large healthcare provider that transitioned to a cloud-based infrastructure to support the backend of its patient management systems. Legacy systems struggled to integrate new applications and handle increasing data loads, leading to significant inefficiencies and slow response times. The organization adopted a hybrid cloud strategy, implementing Amazon Web Services (AWS) alongside on-premises resources to enhance scalability and responsiveness.

Central to this transition was the introduction of Amazon Elastic Kubernetes Service (EKS), allowing for seamless deployment and management of containerized applications in a scalable environment. The organization designed automated scaling rules based on patient data and request volumes, which ensured that application instances adjusted dynamically based on usage patterns. Previously, resource allocation was static and insufficient during peak hours; however, with EKS, the organization achieved continuous performance without experiencing downtimes.

The integration of AWS CloudWatch enabled the team to establish comprehensive monitoring for application performance and resource utilization. Regular audits and performance reviews identified opportunities for optimization, including custom review processes around backup, security, and maintenance. Ultimately, the migration culminated in improved patient data management and operational efficiency.

In contrast, a third case study highlights a financial institution that faced significant technical debt due to inefficient legacy processes. The organization utilized virtual machines (VMs) extensively but found that the resource overhead was unmanageable, impacting service delivery and raising operational costs. To address these issues, the team embarked on a project to migrate systems to a containerized architecture, leveraging an open-source orchestration tool for streamlined management.

The transition to a microservices architecture allowed for enhanced resource utilization while maintaining the requisite compliance and security requirements critical for the financial industry. Initially, services were migrated incrementally, with extensive testing to ensure compatibility and reliability. This meticulous approach minimized risk and allowed the organization to transition without disrupting existing operations.

Furthermore, the new architecture improved the organization's ability to handle transactions with scalability and speed, driven by automatic scaling features integrated into the container management platform. The organization utilized real-time monitoring to assess transaction performance and identify any process bottlenecks. Regular logging and analysis of transaction handling processes facilitated continuous improvement.

Finally, the financial institution leveraged analytics to assess user patterns, leading to better forecasting of infrastructure needs. This data-driven approach enabled the team to adapt their resources intelligently, ensuring they could accommodate peaks in transactions with speed and efficiency—enhancing the reliability of their financial services while minimizing operational costs.

In conclusion, these case studies underline the integral role of strategic planning, modern architecture adoption, and proactive response mechanisms in achieving scalability success in Linux environments. Each organization faced unique challenges and, through adaptive strategies including containerization, hybrid cloud solutions, thorough resource monitoring, and continuous improvements, they effectively navigated these complexities. As you reflect on these examples, consider how effectively integrating process management principles can help foster a resilient Linux environment capable of meeting evolving business needs and user demands.

18. Automating Process Management

18.1. Automation Tools and Scripts

Automation Tools and Scripts

In today's fast-paced IT landscape, automation has emerged as a cornerstone of effective process management in Linux environments. As system administrators grapple with the increasing complexity associated with managing multiple processes, automation tools and scripts offer invaluable capabilities that streamline operations and enhance overall efficiency. Mastering automation empowers administrators to minimize manual workloads, reduce human errors, and maintain responsive systems that can adapt to changing demands.

At the forefront of automation in Linux process management are a variety of tools designed to facilitate seamless integration and management of tasks. One such tool is Ansible, an open-source automation platform known for its simplicity, flexibility, and agentless architecture. Administrators can define playbooks—structured scripts that outline the desired states of system processes—allowing for the automated deployment, management, and configuration of processes across multiple servers. This capability not only accelerates deployment times but also ensures that processes are consistently managed regardless of the underlying infrastructure.

Bash scripts, on the other hand, provide an accessible and powerful means of automating tasks at a granular level. Administrators can create custom scripts that perform actions such as monitoring process states, sending alerts based on resource usage thresholds, or performing routine clean-ups of ephemeral processes. A simple Bash script can be scheduled to run at specific intervals using cron, offering a straightforward method for ongoing process management:

```bash
\#!/bin/bash

\# Check for idle processes and terminate them
for pid in $(ps -eo pid,etime | awk '$2 ~ /[0-9]+:00/ {print $1}'); do
```

```
    echo "Terminating idle process: $pid"
    kill $pid
done
```

This snippet identifies processes that have been running for a specified duration and terminates them, thus preventing resource wastage.

For more comprehensive automation, consider tools like Jenkins for continuous integration and continuous deployment (CI/CD). Jenkins facilitates automated deployment processes, ensuring that applications are deployed consistently while maintaining visibility over build and test stages. This integration of automation into development workflows fosters a seamless transition between environments, reducing the likelihood of errors that could arise during manual deployments.

Kubernetes stands out as a powerful orchestration tool that not only manages containerized applications but also automates scaling and management of processes as demand fluctuates. Kubernetes utilizes features like Horizontal Pod Autoscalar to automatically scale the number of container instances based on predefined metrics, enhancing responsiveness without requiring human intervention. This capability is particularly invaluable in environments where resource demands can change unpredictably, ensuring that processes operate efficiently at all times.

Monitoring automated processes becomes essential to maintaining reliability and accuracy. Advanced monitoring solutions, such as Prometheus and Grafana, offer powerful visualization capabilities, allowing administrators to track the performance of automated tasks in real-time. Regular evaluation of performance data helps identify anomalies in automated processes, enabling swift intervention if issues arise. Coupling automated monitoring scripts with alerting mechanisms ensures administrators remain informed of the state of their processes.

While automation is often celebrated for its capabilities, it is crucial to find the right balance between automated and manual oversight.

Over-reliance on automation can obscure visibility into critical processes, potentially making it difficult to troubleshoot and respond to issues when they arise. A hybrid approach that leverages automation while maintaining manual oversight allows administrators to benefit from the efficiency of automation while still being able to assess and intervene as necessary.

Lastly, the future of automation in process management is set to be influenced by emerging trends, such as the continued integration of artificial intelligence and machine learning. As these technologies evolve, they promise to enhance the capabilities of automation tools, allowing systems to intelligently adapt and respond to changing conditions without administrator intervention. This paradigm shift will empower organizations to optimize their processes and enhance overall performance, creating a responsive ecosystem that can thrive amidst the complexities of modern computing.

In summary, automation tools and scripts are integral to optimizing process management in Linux environments. By leveraging platforms such as Ansible, Jenkins, and Kubernetes, alongside custom scripting in Bash, administrators can streamline workflows and enhance resource management. Effective monitoring practices ensure that automated processes remain reliable and responsive to resources, while careful balancing between automation and human oversight fosters a cohesive operational dynamic. As advancements continue to unfold, embracing automation will prove essential to cultivating a resilient and efficient Linux environment—much like skilled horticulturists nurture every facet of their botanical masterpieces to ensure flourishing growth.

18.2. Scheduling and Automation Frameworks

In the realm of system administration, where commands become spells that conjure optimally running servers, mastering the process tree on a Linux system is akin to perfecting the art of bonsai. Just as the bonsai artist carefully trims branches to shape a healthy and aesthetically pleasing miniature tree, so too must a system administrator understand, monitor, and, when necessary, kill processes to maintain an efficient and stable operating environment. But why delve into the intricate dance of threads, memory allocations, and runtime binaries?

Imagine a maze of operations, each path leading to tasks as diverse as handling user requests, processing computations, and managing network traffic. Within this labyrinth, 'Top' emerges as the magical lens, providing a dynamic, real-time view of these concurrent processes. Although 'Top' is fundamentally a powerful snapshot of system activity, the wisdom lies in knowing how to wield its capabilities effectively, pruning away unnecessary processes while nurturing those critical to your server's mission.

This book embarks on a journey through the Linux process tree, a quest not just to harness 'Top' but to transcend its basic use, equipping you with the knowledge to sculpt a responsive, agile system. As you navigate through chapters packed with technical insights, practical guides, and theoretical foundations, you will discover the elegance and necessity of mastery in process management, transforming complexity into simplicity. In your hands, the art of process-pruning will become as second nature as tending to a bonsai, and the Linux system will be your flourishing masterpiece.

Scheduling and Automation Frameworks

A critical aspect of effective process management is establishing and embracing scheduling and automation frameworks. These frameworks enable system administrators to ensure that resources are utilized efficiently, tasks are executed promptly, and responses to system events are automated. As organizations evolve and rely increasingly on consistent and reliable infrastructure, implementing robust scheduling and automation becomes indispensable.

Finding the right scheduling framework begins with assessing the specific needs of your environment. Tools like `cron` and `systemd timers` offer scheduling capabilities that allow administrators to automate the execution of scripts or commands at predefined intervals or specific times. With `cron`, administrators can create simple entries in the crontab file specifying when and how often commands should run, making it straightforward to automate routine tasks such as backups, report generation, and process monitoring.

For example, a scheduled backup script can be easily set to run every day at midnight using the following crontab entry:

```
0 0 * * * /path/to/backup_script.sh
```

On the other hand, `systemd` timers offer more complex scheduling capabilities, capable of handling tasks based on event triggers and system states. By defining timer units within systemd, administrators can create robust scheduling mechanisms that suit their operational requirements. For instance, a systemd timer can trigger a service based on system startup or inactivity, allowing for more adaptive automation workflows.

Scripting languages play a pivotal role in automation frameworks, enhancing the capabilities of scheduling tools. By writing Bash or Python scripts, administrators can implement detailed logic surrounding process management and manipulation. These scripts provide the flexibility to monitor resource usage, fetch status updates of critical services, and even trigger alerts if specific conditions are met.

For example, a straightforward script may be created to check the health of a web server after each startup, ensuring it is running correctly and meets performance requirements:

```
\#!/bin/bash

if systemctl is-active --quiet my_web_server; then
    echo "Web server is running."
else
    systemctl start my_web_server
    echo "Web server started."
fi
```

In an enterprise context, integrating more sophisticated automation frameworks like Ansible or Puppet can significantly enhance scheduling and management. These tools facilitate orchestrating intricate workflows across numerous servers and services, allowing process management practices to be applied consistently across the environment. They enable administrators to define and enforce configurations, automate deployments, and streamline updates, ensuring a cohesive approach to process orchestration.

Moreover, as organizations shift toward containerization and microservices architectures, adapting scheduling frameworks accordingly is essential. Utilizing tools such as Kubernetes allows administrators to define resource requirements and establish automatic scaling based on system load, efficiently distributing tasks among available containers. Kubernetes can automatically manage workload distributions and service health checks via defined policies, heralding a new era of intelligent and responsive process management.

To ensure the reliability and accuracy of scheduled and automated processes, consistent monitoring practices must be integrated. Implementing logging and error reporting solutions facilitates tracking the outcomes of scheduled tasks and allows administrators to diagnose issues quickly. Tools such as Syslog or ELK stack can help visualize and aggregate logs while providing insights into anomalies that may occur due to automation or scheduled tasks.

Finding the right balance between automation and manual oversight is essential for maintaining effective process management. While automating repetitive tasks enhances efficiency, human intervention remains crucial when facing complex or unprecedented situations. Ensuring a clear communication channel among team members will lead to better management of processes while also nurturing a culture of collaboration in overall operations.

In summary, scheduling and automation frameworks are essential to optimizing process management in Linux systems. By utilizing tools like `cron`, `systemd`, and advanced automation frameworks such as Ansible or Kubernetes, administrators can create robust, efficient workflows that enhance system performance and reliability. Furthermore, ensuring proper monitoring and establishing a collaborative culture around process management helps preserve the delicate balance of automation and oversight, ultimately leading to flourishing and responsive Linux environments, much like the meticulous craftsmanship that results in a beautifully shaped bonsai. Properly executed, these practices will empower administrators to anticipate workload demands and respond dynamically to maintain a harmonious operating environment.

18.3. Monitoring Automated Processes

Monitoring automated processes is crucial in maintaining a healthy operational environment in Linux systems. With the proliferation of automated scripts and processes, ensuring reliability and accuracy in these automations requires diligent oversight and continuous monitoring. This aspect of process management helps administrators proactively manage potential disruptions, optimize resource utilization, and enhance overall system performance.

To begin, the first step in monitoring automated processes is establishing clear performance metrics that define the expected behavior of each process. These metrics can include resource utilization percentages (such as CPU and memory), response times, error rates, and completion times for specific tasks. By clearly defining what successful execution looks like, administrators can identify anomalies when processes deviate from these norms.

Utilizing monitoring tools can significantly enhance the ability to track and assess automated processes in real-time. Tools such as Nagios, Prometheus, and Zabbix provide comprehensive monitoring capabilities, allowing administrators to set alerts when defined thresholds are crossed. For example, an alert may trigger if a scheduled backup process takes longer than usual to complete, indicating a potential issue that requires immediate attention.

Logs generated by automated processes also serve as vital sources of information for monitoring. Regularly reviewing these logs through tools like `journalctl` or a centralized logging solution such as the ELK stack allows administrators to gain insights into the execution history of automated tasks. Analyzing logs can reveal recurrent errors, inconsistencies, or failures, enabling administrators to take proactive measures before these issues escalate.

Additionally, implementing automated health checks for critical processes is an effective strategy for monitoring. Scripts can be designed to verify the status of automated tasks after execution to ensure they completed successfully. For example, a script that verifies the outcome of a scheduled database backup could check for the existence of a log file or a specific success message in the output. By integrating health checks into the automation workflows, administrators can ensure that processes are operating as intended.

When issues arise, a well-structured diagnosis pathway is essential. Established frameworks for handling process failures can streamline the investigation, ensuring that administrators are equipped to respond quickly. Documenting the specific behaviors and expected outcomes for each automated process enhances clarity, guiding administrators towards efficient troubleshooting techniques when deviations occur.

Balancing automation with manual oversight is also an essential consideration in monitoring automated processes. While automation reduces the manual workload and increases efficiency, maintaining human involvement is crucial, especially for complex systems. Administrators should reserve specific time to review automated processes periodically, assessing their performance, identifying automation gaps, and making necessary adjustments.

Finally, a culture of continuous improvement should be fostered. Encouraging feedback from users and team members regarding the efficacy of automated processes allows for iterative enhancements. Regular evaluations provide the opportunity to adjust automation strategies, enhance security measures, and refine existing workflows based on practical experiences and observations.

In conclusion, monitoring automated processes is critical for maintaining reliability and performance within Linux environments.

By establishing clear metrics, leveraging robust monitoring tools, utilizing logs for insights, incorporating automated health checks, maintaining a balance with manual oversight, and fostering a culture of continuous improvement, administrators can ensure that their automated processes contribute positively to system operations. This vigilant approach not only enhances efficiency but also empowers administrators to anticipate potential issues, ensuring that automated workflows operate smoothly, akin to the meticulous care employed in managing a flourishing bonsai. Through diligent monitoring, Linux environments can thrive robustly, adapting dynamically to changing workloads and demands.

18.4. Balancing Automation and Manual Oversight

Balancing automation and manual oversight within the context of Linux process management is a delicate exercise that requires an understanding of the strengths and limitations of both approaches. As Linux environments grow in complexity and the demands on processes increase, the integration of automation can significantly enhance efficiency, allowing system administrators to focus on higher-level objectives. However, relying solely on automation can introduce risks, particularly when unexpected issues arise that require human judgment and expertise.

Automation excels at performing routine tasks consistently and efficiently. For instance, automating backups, resource allocation adjustments, and system updates using tools like Ansible or cron scripts allows for uninterrupted processes, reducing the risk of human error. Automation can also enhance responsiveness, enabling systems to adjust dynamically to changing workloads and optimize resources without manual intervention. For example, container orchestration tools like Kubernetes can automatically scale applications based on demand, distributing resources appropriately.

However, while automation provides significant advantages, it should not eliminate the necessity for manual oversight. Automated processes are only as reliable as the scripts and systems that support them. Issues can arise from unanticipated interactions between automated tasks, leading to unintended consequences such as resource contention or application downtimes. In such cases, administrators need to be vigilant in monitoring automated processes for signs of abnormal behavior. By establishing a framework for logging and alerting, administrators can receive real-time notifications about the status of automated tasks, enabling prompt human intervention when necessary.

Moreover, the integration of manual oversight enhances the adaptability and resilience of processes. System administrators bring invaluable experience and insights that can supplement automated processes. While algorithms can effectively follow rules and execute commands, human intuition and critical thinking are critical when diagnosing complex issues that fall outside predictable parameters. By retaining a hands-on approach to crucial processes, administrators can identify areas for improvement, refine workflows, and control potential risks associated with automatically executed tasks.

For optimal balancing, organizations should strive to cultivate a symbiotic relationship between automation and manual processes. This involves integrating automated solutions that enhance process efficiency while establishing regular reviews and monitoring practices to oversee their functionality. System administrators should periodically evaluate automated processes, assessing their performance and results against predetermined benchmarks, and adjusting as necessary. Incorporating predictive analytics into automation allows for the dynamic alignment of resources based on historical performance and anticipated needs, creating a responsive environment that minimizes reliance on manual oversight.

Additionally, ongoing training and education for administrators should be prioritized. As technology evolves, administrators must adapt by acquiring skills in automation tools, scripts, and monitoring practices while remaining well-versed in the underlying systems they manage. This dual expertise enables administrators to bridge the gap between automation and manual oversight effectively, ensuring that automation is employed strategically to enhance overall process management.

In conclusion, maintaining a balance between automation and manual oversight in Linux process management is essential for achieving optimal efficiency and responsiveness. By leveraging the advantages of automation while retaining a human touch in monitoring and decision-making, system administrators can cultivate robust, resilient environments capable of meeting the demands of modern computing. Much like the meticulous care required to tend a bonsai tree, this balance ensures that processes not only thrive but are also nurtured in a way that supports long-term operational vitality. Embracing both automation and manual oversight as complementary strategies will lead to more effective process management practices, ultimately enhancing overall system performance and user satisfaction.

18.5. The Future of Automation in Process Management

The rapid advancement of automation in process management reflects the increasing demand for efficiency, performance, and reliability in modern IT environments. As organizations migrate toward more dynamic infrastructures, the future of automation in process management is poised to significantly shape the landscape of Linux systems. This subchapter examines the anticipated evolution of process automation, the technologies that will drive these changes, and the implications for system administrators who navigate and manage Linux processes.

One of the most significant trends is the integration of artificial intelligence (AI) and machine learning (ML) into process management systems. The use of these technologies allows for the analysis of vast amounts of performance data, enabling predictive capabilities that can forecast resource demands and optimize configuration choices dynamically. For instance, AI-powered monitoring tools can identify patterns in process performance over time, advising on adjustments to resource allocations before users even experience performance degradation. This proactive approach to automation forms a key part of future-ready Linux environments.

Moreover, the integration of advanced orchestration platforms will continue to grow in importance. Tools such as Kubernetes are already revolutionizing how applications are deployed and managed in containerized environments, enabling administrators to automate scaling, updates, and failover tasks seamlessly. As organizations increasingly adopt microservices architectures, embracing orchestration will be critical to balancing the demands of complex applications and ensuring that processes run optimally across various containers and cloud environments.

Another area of growth involves automation on the infrastructure level. Infrastructure as Code (IaC) is gaining momentum, allowing organizations to manage system configurations and deployments programmatically. This strategy streamlines tasks like environment provisioning and application deployment, freeing up administrators to focus on higher-level management and strategic tasks. Tools such as Terraform and CloudFormation provide robust capabilities for creating and managing cloud infrastructure, ensuring that resources are allocated efficiently based on defined configurations and performance needs.

As the reliance on cloud infrastructure increases, organizations must also adapt their process management strategies to accommodate hybrid and multi-cloud environments. Future automation frameworks will require robust mechanisms for managing processes across various platforms, ensuring consistency and reliability. The ability to transfer workloads seamlessly between on-premises and cloud environments will be crucial for optimizing resource utilization and maintaining operational efficiency.

In tandem with these trends, there will be a heightened emphasis on security and compliance in automation strategies. As systems become more automated, the potential attack surface also increases, necessitating stringent security controls. Automation tools should be designed to enforce security policies while facilitating compliance with industry regulations. This entails embedding security checks into automation workflows, ensuring that processes not only operate efficiently but also adhere to security best practices.

Another factor influencing the future of automation in process management is the ongoing need for user-centric design. As process management increasingly becomes automated, tools and interfaces must be user-friendly to allow administrators to implement and monitor automation solutions effectively. Emphasizing transparency in monitoring systems will empower users to understand what is happening under the hood, ultimately fostering a collaborative and responsive operational culture.

Finally, responding to the increasing pace of technological change requires an adaptive mindset among system administrators. Continuous learning and professional development will be essential as new tools, methodologies, and practices emerge. Embracing certification programs, training courses, and community engagement will help administrators stay relevant and proficient in navigating future advancements in automation and process management.

In conclusion, the future of automation in process management is shaped by emerging technologies, evolving methodologies, and an unwavering focus on efficiency, security, and user experience. By harnessing AI and ML, embracing orchestration platforms, implementing Infrastructure as Code, prioritizing security, and committing to continuous learning, organizations can cultivate agile environments where processes flourish autonomously, aligned closely with business goals. As we look to the future, effective automation will ultimately allow Linux systems to thrive, adapting dynamically to the ever-evolving landscape of modern technology. This evolution reflects the delicate balance sought in the world of bonsai cultivation, where every decision can enhance the art and performance of the whole creation.

19. The Future of Linux Process Management

19.1. Emerging Trends and Technologies

As we look toward the future of Linux process management, several emerging trends and technologies stand poised to transform how system administrators approach their roles in an increasingly complex digital landscape. The rapid evolution of technology necessitates a robust understanding of these trends to adapt effectively, ensuring the continued efficiency and security of Linux systems.

One key trend is the growing adoption of containerization technologies, primarily driven by platforms such as Docker and Kubernetes. Containerization enhances process management by enabling applications to run in isolated environments that contain all necessary dependencies. This approach offers agility, scalability, and efficiency, making it particularly appealing for organizations looking to streamline deployments and optimize resource utilization. As organizations increasingly operate on microservices architectures, proficiency in managing containers will become essential for assuring seamless interactions among processes.

Another important trend is the integration of artificial intelligence (AI) and machine learning (ML) into process management. These technologies facilitate the automatic analysis of system performance data, enabling predictive adjustments to resource allocations and proactive identification of potential issues. For example, systems that analyze historical resource usage patterns can self-optimize in real-time, dynamically allocating CPU or memory based on anticipated demands. Embracing AI-driven strategies will pave the way for agile and responsive Linux environments, ultimately enhancing performance and user satisfaction.

The continuous shift towards cloud computing and hybrid infrastructures further influences the future of Linux process management. As businesses embrace cloud solutions, administrators will need to develop strategies for managing processes that span multiple environments, ensuring consistent and efficient operations across on-premises and cloud-based resources. Mastery of cloud-native tools and orchestration platforms will be paramount for professionals navigating this landscape, requiring investment in skills that facilitate the effective management of resources across diverse infrastructures.

As the complexities of process management grow, the emphasis on security cannot be understated. With an increase in cyber threats targeting vulnerabilities in processes, robust security frameworks will be essential to protect systems. Technologies such as SELinux and AppArmor, which provide granular access controls, will be fundamental for ensuring that processes operate securely within their designated environments. The future will demand that administrators develop a strong foundation in security best practices, integrating these considerations into all elements of process management.

In the face of constant advancements in technology, adapting to change will be critical for systems administrators. Continued professional development through training, certification, and community engagement will become vital for maintaining relevance in a rapidly evolving field. Embracing opportunities for learning—be it through online courses, industry conferences, or knowledge-sharing sessions —will empower professionals to navigate new tools and methodologies effectively.

Finally, system administrators must anticipate unforeseen challenges that may arise as technologies evolve. Exploring contingency planning, incident response strategies, and ongoing monitoring practices will be essential for mitigating potential dysfunctions in process management. Engaging in post-incident reviews will provide insights into how processes performed under different conditions and shape future preparedness efforts.

In conclusion, the future of Linux process management is characterized by the rapid pace of technological evolution, emphasizing the importance of adaptability, security, and ongoing professional development. By staying informed of emerging trends such as containerization, AI integration, and cloud-native strategies, system administrators can position themselves to thrive amid these changes. Cultivating a mindset geared toward continuous improvement and preparedness will ensure that Linux environments flourish, effectively balancing performance and resilience akin to the meticulous care required in nurturing a finely shaped bonsai tree. As these trends unfold, embracing them will empower administrators to optimize process management and contribute to the broader operational success of their organizations.

19.2. Linux in Modern IT Infrastructure

In the vast landscape of modern IT infrastructure, Linux has secured its position as a foundational operating system, underpinning a myriad of enterprises, cloud solutions, and hypervisors. Its stability, flexibility, and versatility have made it a popular choice for managing everything from servers and containers to cybersecurity applications. Understanding the integral role of Linux in shaping modern infrastructures is crucial for system administrators, developers, and IT professionals alike.

Linux's architecture allows for the implementation of robust and reliable systems capable of handling significant workloads with efficiency. For instance, Linux servers are extensively deployed in data centers, supporting applications that require high availability and resource scalability. This ability to scale makes Linux an ideal candidate for cloud computing models, where resources must be provisioned and managed dynamically based on demand. Platforms like Amazon Web Services (AWS), Google Cloud Platform (GCP), and Microsoft Azure all leverage Linux to support their infrastructures, utilizing its performance and reliability to deliver customer solutions at scale.

Moreover, the rise of containerization technologies, such as Docker and orchestration platforms like Kubernetes, has further solidified Linux's relevance in modern IT environments. Containers, powered by Linux's capabilities, allow applications to be run in isolated environments without the overhead of traditional virtualization. This leads to improved resource allocation, faster deployment times, and enhanced process management capabilities. As organizations shift toward microservices architectures, Linux's ability to facilitate efficient container management is paramount to achieving operational excellence.

Additionally, with the growing emphasis on security in modern infrastructures, Linux continues to adapt and evolve. Advanced security measures, such as SELinux or AppArmor, offer robust access controls that ensure processes operate within predefined security boundaries. Coupled with tools for monitoring and logging, administrators can detect anomalies and act promptly to mitigate risks associated with process management.

As enterprises increasingly move toward cloud-native solutions, Linux plays a critical role in streamlining software development and deployment processes. The adoption of DevOps practices, which emphasize collaboration between development and operations, often revolves around Linux tools and environments. From CI/CD pipelines to automated testing frameworks, Linux facilitates efficient workflows that drive innovation and speed to market.

However, while Linux provides a strong foundation for modern infrastructures, adapting to technological changes is equally essential for IT professionals. Continuous learning and agility in adopting new tools and methodologies are crucial in keeping pace with the rapidly evolving landscape. Emerging technologies—such as artificial intelligence, machine learning, and hybrid cloud integrations—are requiring system administrators to refine their skills continually, ensuring that they remain equipped to handle both current and future challenges.

Furthermore, organizations must be prepared to confront unforeseen challenges as they navigate their technological journeys. From addressing sudden spikes in resource demand to managing security breaches, the ability to anticipate potential disruptions and implement effective solutions is paramount. Employing a proactive approach that incorporates real-time monitoring, automation, and disaster recovery planning can significantly mitigate risks, ensuring operational continuity in turbulent times.

Finally, investing in skill development related to process management is vital for long-term success. Understanding the intricacies of Linux process management—from resource allocation and optimization to security and performance monitoring—will provide a significant competitive advantage. Engaging in professional development through training, certification programs, and community involvement fosters a culture of continuous improvement that benefits both individuals and organizations.

In conclusion, Linux's role in modern IT infrastructure is multidimensional, influencing everything from application deployment to security. By embracing the opportunities provided by Linux while continuously adapting to technological changes and preparing for potential challenges, system administrators can cultivate resilient systems that support day-to-day operations effectively. This agile mindset not only positions organizations for successful navigation through the ever-evolving landscape but also fosters professional growth and reliability in process management practices. As these advancements unfold, investing in skills that align with the future of Linux and process management will ensure ongoing excellence in the enterprise infrastructure landscape.

19.3. Adapting to Technological Change

Navigating the vast and dynamic landscape of technology, particularly in the realm of Linux process management, necessitates a proactive approach to adapting to technological change. As systems evolve, new tools and methodologies emerge, challenging administrators to stay ahead of the curve and continuously enhance their skills. This section outlines the key considerations in adapting to technological change and the strategies that can be employed to foster professional growth in process management.

One of the primary considerations in adapting to technological change is the importance of continual learning. Technology is in a constant state of flux, with new frameworks, tools, and best practices emerging seemingly every day. To remain effective, Linux administrators must cultivate a mentality of lifelong learning. Engaging with online courses, attending workshops and conferences, and participating in professional communities contribute to a robust learning experience. Various platforms, such as Coursera, Udemy, and Linux Academy, offer specialized training focused on process management and system administration, allowing individuals to adapt their skill sets concurrently with emerging technologies.

Additionally, staying connected with industry news and trends is vital for understanding technological advances that might impact process management. Subscribing to relevant blogs, academic publications, or news feeds keeps administrators informed about new developments, helping them anticipate adjustments that may be necessary in their environments. Engaging with communities on forums like Reddit, Stack Exchange, or specialized Linux user groups can facilitate knowledge sharing, exposing administrators to real-world scenarios and solutions from professionals facing similar challenges.

Another critical area of focus is the exploration of automation tools and techniques. Understanding the capabilities of configuration management systems like Ansible, Puppet, or Chef—along with monitoring solutions like Prometheus and Grafana—empowers administrators to streamline process management significantly. By mastering these tools, administrators can automate routine tasks, monitor processes proactively, and optimize resource allocations, contributing to system resilience and operational efficiency.

In addition to technical skills, developing strong problem-solving abilities is essential in adapting to technological change. The capacity to identify issues, analyze root causes, and implement effective solutions is invaluable when faced with unexpected challenges. Engaging in practice scenarios, such as simulated disaster recovery drills or troubleshooting exercises, allows administrators to refine their approach to problem resolution while building confidence in their capabilities.

As organizations increasingly adopt cloud technologies, adapting to environments that include hybrid and multi-cloud infrastructures becomes paramount. Familiarity with cloud computing platforms—such as AWS, Azure, or Google Cloud—will become indispensable when managing processes distributed across various environments. Understanding their respective resource management, security configurations, and orchestration opportunities will help administrators leverage cloud capabilities effectively.

To prepare for unforeseen challenges, organizations must cultivate a culture characterized by adaptability and agile response strategies. Formulating incident response plans that outline the necessary steps to take in the event of process failures, security breaches, or resource shortages is essential. Regularly reviewing and updating these plans ensures that they retain relevance and that team members are aware of their roles and responsibilities during critical incidents.

In conclusion, adapting to technological change, growing skills in process management, and preparing for unforeseen challenges are intertwined elements crucial for success in Linux environments. By embracing a mindset of lifelong learning, staying connected with industry developments, mastering automation tools, refining problem-solving capabilities, and formulating robust incident response strategies, Linux administrators can position themselves to thrive amidst evolving technology landscapes. This proactive approach enables them to manage processes effectively, ensuring operational efficiency and resilience in their organizations as they navigate the complexities of modern computing. As practitioners refine their skills, the art of process management transforms into a seamless orchestration that cultivates robust systems poised for success, reminiscent of the meticulous care required in cultivating a flourishing bonsai tree.

19.4. Growing Your Skills in Process Management

In the realm of system administration, mastering process management extends beyond merely monitoring and controlling processes; it encompasses a commitment to continuous learning, adaptation, and proactive management strategies. In this subchapter, we will delve into the strategies you can employ to grow your skills in process management, equipping you with the necessary tools to navigate the complexities of process dynamics in Linux environments.

The first step in developing your skills is to immerse yourself in the fundamental concepts of Linux process management. A solid understanding of how processes operate, their lifecycle stages, how they interact with system resources, and how they relate to one another lays the groundwork for effective management. Consider enrolling in courses focused on Linux administration and process management, provided by platforms such as Coursera or Linux Academy. These courses often incorporate hands-on lab exercises that reinforce your understanding of key concepts.

Next, embrace the vast array of tools available for managing processes. Familiarize yourself with the intricacies of command-line utilities like 'top,' 'htop,' and 'ps' for real-time monitoring, alongside advanced diagnostic tools like `perf`, `strace`, and `valgrind`. Finding time to practice using these tools in a sandbox environment or virtual lab will not only improve your proficiency but will also enhance your comfort in interpreting the data presented, making you more effective in troubleshooting and optimizing processes in your environment.

The implementation of automation in process management cannot be overstated. Learning to automate routine tasks through scripting —using Bash, Python, or automation frameworks like Ansible—will significantly enhance your efficiency as a Linux administrator. Begin by identifying repetitive tasks, then create and refine scripts that automate these processes. The experience gained will deepen your understanding of both the functionality of processes and how to leverage automation to relieve some of the administrative burdens.

Consider becoming engaged in community forums and user groups focused on Linux and open-source technologies. Platforms like Reddit and Stack Overflow provide opportunities to ask questions, share experiences, and learn from peers with varying levels of expertise. Participating in discussions can reveal new techniques and perspectives on process management that may not be covered in traditional courses.

Furthermore, real-world experience is invaluable. Actively seek opportunities to apply your skills in practical contexts, whether through internships, volunteer projects, or contributing to open-source initiatives. Exposure to real-world processes, problems, and solutions will deepen your understanding of how process management fits within the broader organizational framework.

Understanding modern trends in process management is equally essential. Keep abreast of developments such as containerization technologies (e.g., Docker, Kubernetes), cloud computing, and the integration of AI-driven analytics into process management. Engaging with these evolving trends will prepare you to implement the latest best practices and enhance your organization's operational resilience.

Additionally, continuous assessment of your skills is vital for growth. Set specific goals for your learning, such as mastering automation tools or diving into advanced performance monitoring techniques. Regularly assess your progress, seek feedback, and recalibrate your learning path as needed. Engaging in self-reflection allows you to identify areas where you excel and those requiring further attention, thereby guiding your development efforts.

Finally, don't underestimate the importance of building a strong professional network. Collaborate with fellow administrators, developers, and security professionals to share insights and challenges you've encountered in process management. Strong networks often lead to mentorship opportunities, which can provide invaluable guidance as you develop your skills and navigate complex systems.

In summary, growing your skills in process management requires a multifaceted approach that encompasses education, tool familiarity, automation, real-world experience, trend awareness, continuous assessment, and networking. By committing to these strategies, you will deepen your understanding of process dynamics within Linux systems, enabling you to manage processes effectively and cultivate a thriving operational environment. Just as a bonsai artist learns to shape each part of their creation for optimal growth, you will refine your skills and knowledge to nurture a finely-tuned Linux process management system that delivers efficiency and reliability. As you journey through this professional development, embrace opportunities for growth that prepare you to meet present and future challenges within your Linux environments.

19.5. Unforeseen Challenges and Their Solutions

In the realm of Linux process management, and indeed in all domains of system administration, unforeseen challenges can arise that disrupt even the most meticulously planned operations. These challenges can stem from a variety of sources—ranging from hardware failures, network issues, and software bugs to changes in workload demands, resource contention, and security vulnerabilities. Understanding how to identify these challenges and implement effective solutions is essential for maintaining system integrity and performance.

One common unforeseen challenge is the sudden emergence of resource contention, where multiple processes compete for limited system resources such as CPU, memory, or I/O bandwidth. This contention can lead to performance degradation, application timeouts, and user frustration. To address this, administrators should monitor resource usage actively and consider implementing control groups (cgroups) to limit resource consumption by specific processes. By applying these constraints judiciously, critical processes can be prioritized, ensuring that they remain responsive under heavy load conditions.

A related challenge arises from unexpected spikes in workload. For instance, a web application may experience a surge in traffic due to a marketing campaign or a news event, overwhelming the system's resources. In such cases, automated scaling solutions—like Kubernetes or cloud-based autoscaling features—can dynamically adjust resource allocations in response to real-time demand. These solutions enable organizations to scale their infrastructure up or down efficiently while ensuring that performance remains optimal, even during peak usage scenarios.

Software bugs and application-level issues can also surface unexpectedly, leading to crashes or erratic process behavior. Such situations necessitate robust diagnostic tools for troubleshooting. Tools like `strace`, `perf`, and `gdb` allow administrators to analyze system calls, monitor resource usage, and perform post-mortem analyses on crashed processes. Incorporating thorough logging practices using tools like `syslog` or the `journalctl` command helps administrators capture contextual information leading up to failures, which is invaluable for identifying root causes and implementing long-term fixes.

Network issues often emerge as unforeseen challenges, particularly in systems relying on inter-process communication. Latency, packet loss, and bandwidth limitations can all hinder processes from operating effectively. Employing tools such as `ping`, `traceroute`, and `iftop` helps diagnose network-related problems, enabling administrators to understand network performance and make adjustments accordingly. Additionally, implementing Quality of Service (QoS) measures can help prioritize network traffic for critical processes, ensuring that bandwidth is allocated effectively.

Security vulnerabilities represent another critical area for unforeseen challenges. Malicious attacks may exploit weaknesses within processes, leading to unauthorized access or data breaches. Establishing a robust security posture through techniques such as process isolation, mandatory access controls (e.g., SELinux or AppArmor), and continuous security assessments is essential for mitigating these risks. Regular updates and patch management for software and libraries must also be implemented to protect against known vulnerabilities.

Another challenge that administrators may face is managing dependency conflicts between processes or libraries. As applications evolve, outdated libraries can lead to compatibility issues, resulting in process failures. Regular audits of library versions through tools like `ldd` or `apt-cache policy` can assist in identifying potential conflicts early on. When an issue arises, ensuring that all dependencies are compatible is crucial to restoring application functionality quickly.

In all instances, documentation and proactive communication play an essential role in addressing unforeseen challenges. Creating detailed incident reports outlining the occurring issues, procedures followed, and resulting solutions fosters a knowledge-sharing culture within the team. This repository of information can inform future responses to similar challenges and enhance the overall capacity for systemic resilience.

In conclusion, unforeseen challenges in Linux process management require vigilance, proactive monitoring, and effective response strategies. By implementing measures such as resource control, automated scaling, robust diagnostics, and diligent security practices, administrators can mitigate the impacts of these challenges when they arise. Establishing a culture of documentation and knowledge sharing further equips teams to navigate these challenges adeptly. As organizations embrace the unexpected, they will cultivate resilient systems capable of thriving in the face of adversity—much like a well-tended bonsai that endures and flourishes against the challenges of nature. Embracing this proactive mindset positions administrators to turn challenges into opportunities for growth, enhancing their overall process management strategies.

www.ingramcontent.com/pod-product-compliance
Lightning Source LLC
LaVergne TN
LVHW051320050326
832903LV00031B/3277